THE MATING GAME

••••••••••••••••••••••••
ANITA LAWSON
••••••••••••••••••••••••

Afterwords Ink
P.O. Box 76374
Washington, DC 20013

Visit our website at: www.anitalawson.com

Copyright © 1999 by Anita Lawson
All rights reserved, including the right of reproduction in whole or in part in any form.

Cover designed by Mad Cap Design Group

Manufactured in the U.S.A.

Library of Congress Cataloging in Publication Data
Lawson, Anita
The Mating Game

ISBN

●●●●●●●●●●●●●●●●●●●●●●●●

Warning

This book contains information of an explicit nature, concerning the sexual games that people play and has been rated:

"KR"

for "**K**eepin' it **R**eal"...

Acknowledgements

"Thank YOU!"

Special thanks go to many people who helped with the success of my first book. They made it possible to produce this one. At the top of my list, "big thanks" go to Renee Towell and Andrew Scher for giving me my first opportunities on national television. Special "thanks" go to Snoop Doggy Dogg, George Price and Michael Baisden for endorsing an unknown writer in 1995. I wish to also thank the entire staff and crew of both the Ricki Lake Show and Tempestt for making this adventure fun. Lastly, I want to thank my family and friends for their kind words.

CONTENTS

Chapter		Page
1	Let the Games Begin	1
2	This Is How We Do It	49
3	The Players	99
4	Creeping	154
5	The Rules	182
6	The Art of Lying	209
7	The Danger Zone	243
8	The Winners' Curse	266
9	Winning Ways	298
10	It's Not Over, 'Til It's Over	333

Chapter 1

Let the Games Begin

■ ■ ■

The Game

In the simplistic ritual that most call "dating", an evolution has taken place, converting this practice into a sensuous game of cat and mouse. Some play for sex; some play for money; others play for the joy of the hunt. Yet, everyone must play to get what he or she wants.

It's not dating; it's mating! Dating is to set aside time to be with someone. Mating is to set aside time with a specific goal in mind. The ultimate goal may be for later, although in our time conscious world, most prefer it now! However, whether it's now or later, it's a game and the race is on to get married, have sex, secure a relationship, find pleasure, and get paid. Therefore, we no longer date, we "mate"! And we are all trapped playing this thing, I call, "The Mating Game"!

Mating Tactics

Have you ever stopped to consider the number of ways in which people get picked up? Well, there are many tactical approaches, but the first and oldest is called...

Go Fish:

This is exactly as it sounds. It's jumping into the masses and seeing what you can pull out. There are three methods used predominantly. There's "Bait & Tag", "Bait & Take" and "Hold, Bait, Tag & Switch".

"Bait & Tag" can best be demonstrated in the clubs. This is how it works. You go up to one guy, screen him, get his phone number and you move on to the next guy to do the same all over again. It's exactly as the name implies; you bait them

in and tag (stake your right or claim) them for possible use later. The key word is LATER. You have no intention of securing any of the men or women you've met for a rendezvous tonight. You are accumulating new prospects for use at a later time.

"Bait & Take" is for more immediate use. It is the simple method of finding something you like and claiming him or her for use NOW. You can be in a relationship or not. It doesn't matter.

"Hold, Bait, Tag & Switch" Is what's done when you prefer to be with one guy at a time but for whatever reason you must always have a guy in waiting for you. So, you don't trade in your old model, until you have the new one on hand. Therefore, you hold onto the one you've got, bait the new guy in, and screen him. If that works, then you tag and test him out (kind of like trying on a new suit or a few test-drives in a new car). If it seems to work, you switch: break it off with the old guy and keep the new one. That is what we call "Hold, Bait, Tag & Switch".

Variety Sandwich:
Each person has a list of characteristics that he or she thinks would be the makings of a perfect person. In The Mating Game, it is often hard to find that one person, so what we do is create a substitution which consists of several guys and that's what I call a "Variety Sandwich".

To illustrate, let's say that you are athletic, love to read, enjoy political conversations and love to be romanced. To find one guy that could do all of that would be "Mr. Perfect", right? So, in the absence of Mr. Perfect, you create a "Variety Sandwich". In essence, you find a guy that can fulfill each one of your important needs and you take a little bit (or a little bite) of each one. So, when you feel like a political discussion, you call George (the political science major) and when you feel like going running, you call David (the marathon runner) and when you feel like being romanced, you call Darryl (the romantic). A little bit of each creates your perfect guy and satisfies all of your basic requirements, and this is what we refer to as a "Variety Sandwich".

Hit & Run:
This is a method used by people not wanting to really be in a relationship. For whatever reason, we cannot be sure because there are so many possible explanations. But for whatever reason, this person enjoys the initial hunt, capture and scoring with a person. Once this has happened the hunt begins again with someone new. This is often the method used by a player or someone who is in love with the concept of being hunted (or pursued).

Good, Better, Best:
This is a deviation of the "Go Fish" tactic "Hold, Bait, Tag & Switch". It's the same practice, but on a constant and reoccurring basis. It simply requires trading up. That means whatever you like

about your boyfriend or girlfriend, your next one has to be better. Women are good at this. With each boyfriend, they trade up, finding someone that is more attractive, more intelligent, more wealthy, just more of whatever they find to be important.

There is not really much wrong with doing this, except that sometimes people get caught in a continuous loop, and that's what I call *"the Best of the Last Syndrome"*. That means you have tried to find someone better than what you've got, but the guy you thought was better, turned out not to be. So, you keep coming back to your previous boyfriend (the guy that you consider to be the best of the last). However, generally speaking, this tends to always be a mistake, because if you left him/her because things weren't working out, why would circumstances change now? Unless something really has changed and it typically hasn't, things are going to be the same. So, you find yourself trapped, because you will not permanently let go of this guy you had. He inadvertently becomes your safety net, every time you fail at finding someone better. So, you keep coming back.

You think you can't find anyone better, but the truth is that you have gotten somewhat comfortable with the fact that you still have Mr. Accessible there to take you back each time you come calling. So, the side effect is that you lose time, miss out on great guys or women (because you just give up looking) and you become tied to a mediocre relationship. You find yourself in this situation because you continue to refuse to look at your many options for new guys, new fun, new flings, or new excitement. You become content with memories and old feelings that appear to you to be "as good as it will ever get".

First Come, First Served:
Guys are notorious for doing this on a daily basis. They have their list of women that seem to be fun. They will rank them in the order of preference from one to whatever. And then they start pursuing their number one choice and work their way down the list. They call up their first choice and ask her out. If she says "no", he moves on to his number two pick. If she says no, then he moves on to three and four and five, until someone is available. Therefore, the first one to come to his private party is the first one served and that is "First Come, First Served."

Pickup Methods
Although we have discussed tactics of accumulating mating prospects, we have not discussed the actual method of approach itself. Therefore, let's address that.

Mirage.
This is the preferred method of choice, heavily used by men. This is what we call it when you pretend to be someone other than yourself. You rent a sports car, you wear the only suit you have and you approach women talking about your

penthouse downtown, your summer home in Florida and the mega pile of "dead presidents or Benjamins" (money) that you spend constantly.

This is the man that will later complain about how he's got a superficial woman. And then yell out in anger "Why can't I find a Real Woman!" The best response to people who use this method (to present a fake or superficial person) and then expect to attract a person unconcerned or phased by superficial things came from a woman who had been trapped with this method in a fake relationship. Jennifer a 28-year old native of Chicago said: "Hell that's how you came to me! ...with the big car and the nice suits and the money to spend. That's how you presented yourself to me, and that's what I THOUGHT I had. If you wanted someone who didn't care if you had those things, why did you come to me like THAT? I didn't change who I was. You changed who you were! So, whose fault was THAT!"

Bottom line, men, if you don't want a woman concerned with superficial things, don't approach her in a superficial way. However, despite it all, men do and will continue to anyway. And if you are just trying to have one-night-stand sex, it's not supposed to matter anyway, right? Ironically, enough, the name of the game is "play and be played; use and be used". If you attempt to use someone, you usually are getting used in return yourself. So, I guess what you give is what you get, and if you still continue to use this pickup method then...that's your decision.

One-Mind Method.
This is not an easy method to fake. It's what happens when two people share common interests or share a common passion. It could be anything: a sport, a cause, an attitude, a profession, a hobby, etc. Some men try to pretend, but if you're not a good liar, you can easily get caught. This approach provides a fine line to walk for the bogus.

Don't be fooled, women try to use this method all the time too. Pretending that we love football, when we can't stand it or going to play tennis, when we've never played a game. The irony is that women who are pretending to have that common interest can sometimes get away with it (under the worst of circumstances). The reason is because her lack of knowledge about something of interest to him gives him the opportunity to show his wealth of knowledge or how good he is at a particular sport or hobby. Men love the opportunity to teach and share the love of their favorite sport with someone who is at least slightly interested or attempting to be. Women, as a result, can get away with the grandest of lies under this category, due to the guy's ego or vanity.

However, beware,... if he is a well-grounded individual, then he might see through too much bull shit. So, for the well-grounded guy, you might want to take it easy of the bull. However, for all the rest with big egos and the need to feed them, you can make out like a fat cat, pouring on the damsel in distress act to the big football or tennis star-wannabe, who is only missing one thing: a fan. And, that could be you!

Compliments Galore.
This is almost a guaranteed method for success. The way this works is simple. You constantly compliment your target (prey, subject, whatever you want to call them). Who can resist being showered with compliments? And, if you truly believe the compliments you are dishing, then that makes it all the better!

When targeting a certain special person, find out as much as you can in advance of a meeting. Your sources might include friends, co-workers or documented resources. Whether it is a plaque on his or her office wall or an article that featured this individual, it will all work. There is nothing more FLATTERING than to have someone take the time to find out something about you, before they approach you; you come across in a less superficial way. The main draw back, however, to this method is that it is time consuming. Therefore, it is a method reserved for a special group of people and your prospect knows that...which is another reason why it's even more appealing a method when used.

Man Hunt Method.
While I hate to admit it, some women like the thrill of the hunt and the challenge of the chase. To get something that you are told you can't have or shouldn't have like the bad boy or the sexy guy that

doesn't want a relationship is appealing. And that is what has created the Man Hunt Method. This method means, of course, that the woman is hunting the man. Ironically enough, women have been "the hunted" for years. So, now both sides feel free to hunt each other openly.

The way it works is actually rather simple, compared to the other methods. If the guy has got the looks all he need do is stand back and be hunted. The same is true of the woman. She usually just waits to be approached. Now, there are things that you can do to become more appealing, however, I'll leave that thought for you to be creative with.

However, everyone should recognize that he/she is being watched. There is someone in the club or in the area checking you out to see what kind of person you are. So, you take advantage of that by adding to an illusion, thereby increasing the interest and ultimately prompting people to want to hunt you. These tactics will be discussed in the Chapter entitled "This Is How We Do It!"

What's in a Good Pickup Line

Just as men can smell desperation in a woman, women can smell bull shit in a line. The worst thing to do is to approach a woman with that "Mack Daddy Vibe" (a fake arrogance and old lines that women can smell a mile away). So, what's the best line? The answer is "No, line."

Be Original.
Women hate to hear the same tired lines that are phony and came from someone else.

Imagine that you are an attractive woman who goes out frequently. You are constantly approached. So, you've pretty much heard every line that's out there. And if there's a line that a guy considers to be very good, you can only imagine how many times she's heard it, for obviously the same reason that every guy that approached her thought it was special too. You get the picture, no matter how good you think a line is, it's still a line...

2. *Be Respectful.*
There's nothing more upsetting than a man who is trying to approach you and doesn't even show an ounce of respect, for you as a woman and as an individual.

Imagine: ...you're a man, especially a Black man, and imagine that you are sitting in a diner eating some lunch and an attractive woman walks up to you and says, "Hey, BOY! Come here. I want to TALK to YOU, BOY!! I said, bring it over here NOW!" It doesn't matter how cute she is; you wouldn't appreciate it at all. Because she just DISRESPECTED you, and not only that. She did it in public! Well, that's the way a woman feels when men approach her without giving her respect. There's NO difference! It doesn't matter how FINE he is, if he walks up to a group of women and says, "Hmmm! Okay. Which one can I HAVE?" A man actually said this to a group of women I spoke to. This displays a lack of respect and this was suppose to be his best side. Obviously, it's down hill from here.

3. Be Sincere.
Women are suckers for sincerity. Men that approach them as themselves, rather than as some fake person tend to come across as being real. And if you think about it for a moment, you'll realize that no one is like you. Therefore, by default you will always be an original. So, if you just allow yourself to be yourself, you can't help but be a sincere person coming to a woman from the heart.

4. Be Confident.
Confidence can make the most unattractive man, attractive, and a lack of it can make the most attractive man unappealing VERY quickly. Now, I didn't say arrogant! I said confident. There is a difference. Confidence is being comfortable in your own skin and in your surroundings. Arrogance is to over compensate for a lack of comfort. Arrogance is phony, it's superficial, and it's pretentious.

Male Mating Etiquette
There are some things that really should be spelled out for men. The do's and don'ts of mating (or dating as you may call it). Here are the more important items that men should be aware of.

1. Don't Nest!

Men, you ever wonder why women can be so rude, when all you did was say, "hello"? It's because she is not trying to get saddled with a "Nester", someone who meets you in a club, has nothing in common with you, but hangs around you all night, blocking other potentially interesting guys from coming her way.

She puts on that false arrogant attitude, because she doesn't want to give you the impression that you can stick around. She'll listen for a while, but if she doesn't think that it's going to work out, she wants to know that she can walk away and you will not try to find her later. It's a safety measure, just in case she doesn't want you taking up her time. Remember, men, you are there to find somebody, just like she is. Don't take the fact that she was nice to mean that she wants to have your baby! Know when it's time to step (leave).

2. Don't come to a club or go on a date BROKE!

Women hate a broke-ass man. Now don't get me wrong, a man doesn't have to be rich to have a nice date with a woman. But don't invite her out on a date, make her feel that you've got it all under control and when the bill comes, you stick her with a $225 dinner bill! Hell, she could have taken herself out for half of that and not had to worry about some man that can't even successfully plan out a couple of hours in his life.

You can have limited funds and still date women, but don't take them to the most expensive restaurant in town or to a club and order 2 bottles of their most expensive champagne, only to not have a dime in your pocket. It's just as bad to come up short when you know you should have been prepared. Men who do that on purpose or by mistake, make a woman feel violated.

Men without a lot of money (or who don't want to spend a lot of money) can plan nice dates to the park, to the tennis courts, to a free outdoor concert or to the beach, without making either person feel violated. Two hot-dogs and Cokes are not going to break your wallets, men. Or you can save on the cost of food even more by creating a very nice picnic lunch for the two of you at the park or on the beach. I guarantee you she will be impressed. It is not really about the money, it is about how she is being treated and how you make her feel. Money can do that, but the proper attention can also do it just as well.

3. If you are driving a car on a date, make sure that it is clean and in proper working order.
Now, it's true that some women prefer to be seen in top of the line, luxury cars. But luxury or not, a car should be clean and functional. Picking a woman up in a broken down, non-working car is similar to taking a woman to your apartment and having it filthy and without food or drink to offer. Recognize the importance and take the precautions

to make sure that you don't make her feel unwanted. Because lack of preparation can do that.

4. If you're not going to call a woman and you know this up front, don't build up the expectation that you will.

Men, I cannot tell you how many times I have stayed up nights talking to girlfriends who went out to a club, had a "Bait & Tag" done on them by some guy only to NOT have him call, after he promised he would. Men, I know you don't call every woman you get a phone number from, but do you really need to build up her expectations to anticipate your call the next day? No, you don't. So, don't hype it up and don't make promises you can't keep. Especially, when you are SURE that you are not going call her.

5. Always have clean sheets on your bed, if you intend to invite a woman over to have sex.

This is probably the biggest "MUST" on my list. Men, there is nothing more anti-climactic than to go back to some guy's apartment, get lured into the bedroom and sit on the bed only to discover that his bed sheets are dirty. Men, if you didn't know it before, know it now: CLEAN BED SHEETS ARE A MUST! So, if you are going out clubbing tonight, make sure that you change your bed sheets BEFORE you leave...just in case. Please believe me, few things can kill the prospect of sex like dirty sheets can.

6. When talking to a woman, look at her eyes, not her chest or her ass!

Men, what is this obsession you have with T&A (tits and ass)? If a woman didn't know any better, she would think, this is your first time seeing breasts and booty! If you stop to talk to a woman, talk to her, don't make it an opportunity to see tits and ass up close and personal! Now, don't get me wrong, women like to feel that they look attractive, but that is not what I am talking about. I am talking about a man who during 50% or more of the conversation is talking to a woman's chest and checking out her butt. That is annoying, especially for a woman who has a lot of both. She is not going to be as tolerant, because men are doing that to her all day, everyday. She is not going to stand there while you can't get past your initial fascination. So, talk to the face, because the breasts and the ass ain't hearing you, and CHILL OUT on the rest. Remember, her eyes are in her face, not in her chest.

Female Mating Etiquette

So, what are some of the items women should be aware of when going out clubbing? Here are a few:

1. Acknowledge a guy that is talking to you, even if it's just two words.

Ladies, I know that you don't want to be bothered with about 80% of the men who approach you, but you've got to look at it from the other side too. Each time a man approaches a woman or makes that long, lonely trip across the floor, he has to confront the possibility of being rejected. Now, I am not saying you should sleep with every guy that approaches you or even talk to him all night long, but I DO think that a man who took the time to make an effort warrants at least an acknowledgment of his presence. That could be a few brief sentences of conversation. Again, you don't need to talk to him forever, but a kind acknowledgment, a few words of conversation would not destroy your entire evening.

2. Don't stand in a spot that's hard to get to.

You will not believe how something as small as being in a hard to get to spot can negatively impact your entire evening. For those of you who don't understand, guys go through a weighing process of pros and cons before they approach each woman. And standing in a hard to get to corner can be the item that tips the scales negatively out of your favor and stops you from being approached.

Guys can pass across the floor and act like they were on their way somewhere else, but if you are standing in a corner and he has to go directly to that corner, he can't pretend that he was just passing by. It will be obvious that you were the only reason he headed for the corner and it makes it even worse when he comes out empty handed. Secondly, if he can't reach the spot, then you might as well go home; you aren't going to get any action. So, circulate and don't stand in one corner all night.

3. Walk away from the group of women on occasion.

Just as it is difficult for a woman to approach a man in a very active group, the same is true of a man. Men hesitate to approach a woman if she is out with the ladies on Ladies Night. So, if you want to be approached by a man on Ladies Night or when you're out in a group, break off periodically by yourself. Whether it's to go to the bathroom (by YOURSELF) or to the bar to get a drink, give a guy an opportunity to approach you.

4. Don't drink up all of his money, if you are really not interested in spending time with him.

Men can get nasty about this. We all know, ladies, that most of us go to the clubs with absolutely no intention of spending a dime on drinks, and that's fine. But, if you are just "nesting" with some guy giving him false hope of seeing you again or giving him the false impression that the two of you will have casual sex tonight, just so you can have a few drinks, ...then you know you're wrong. The funny thing is, you are not only cheating him, you're cheating yourself, because you may very well be missing out on some great guy on the other side of the dance floor because you were "nesting" with some guy you never want to see again.

5. Pay for the date sometimes.

This has been brought up many times before in other books, and for good reason. There is a feeling of control in paying for a date. Men feel this power in expecting some sexual payback for their monetary investment of the evening. Women, when you pay for a date, the feeling is, "Okay, we're even". Or in essence, "I don't owe you [him] anything [sex]." It's a good feeling to be able to call the shots, and if the date went well, he could view it as money saved for the opportunity to ask you out again.

6. Be Proactive.

Call him back to say, "thank you" for a date. Don't be afraid to call a guy and invite him out to an event. Men like to see that interest is there on both sides of the table.

7. Don't be difficult.

Guys like intelligent conversation, just like women, but no one wants to be around someone who is not trying to have fun, not trying to be kind and not trying to enjoy your company. Nothing can turn a guy off more than a difficult woman.

8. Postpone, if you don't feel mentally or physically up to a date.

Some guys put a lot of thought and effort into a first date. If you are not in a mood to attempt to enjoy it, you would be doing yourself a favor by postponing.

Despite what you may think, postponing a date will not ruin your chances later (unless it was a casual sex session, in which case the person didn't intend to see you again anyway). When postponing a date, your first impressions have not occurred yet.

The worst thing you could do, is have had wonderful conversations with this guy only to go out on that first date when you're really in a foul mood and mess it up. Because he will think that the person you were on your date (your worst day) is the person you actually are (always).

9. Don't discuss the faults of old boyfriends.

While you may need to talk to someone, because the breakup just occurred, the new guy is NOT the person to talk about it to. While you think you are telling him, don't be this and don't do that. What he is hearing are all of your shortcomings.

If you tell this new guy how your old boyfriend was unfaithful and cheated on you, he doesn't hear "She doesn't take that crap." What he hears is, "Boy, she is gullible." And when you are telling him how you tried to make it work, even though the old boyfriend cheated on you on four separate occasions, he doesn't hear, "She gave all that she could to make it work." What the new guy hears is, "Boy, she's stupid."

Believe me, you are doing the opposite of what you are intending to do. The best way to avoid this problem all together is not discuss the old boyfriend's problems on your date at all.

Who Does He Think I Am?
"Oh, I Think They're Playing My Song"

Have you noticed how music tends to set the tone for a meeting in a club, at a party or during an intimate moment at your place? And have you noticed how your favorite song always appears to have words in it that reflect your current mind set? I'm sure that you have. Art imitates life. An artist doesn't create the slums of New York, when he writes a song about the slums. The slums of New York created the song. He is simply writing about something that already existed. By that same token, have you noticed how closely music has represented how men and women perceive each other over the years? Well, I have. Take a walk with me down memory lane to show how men's images of women have changed.

In the late 60's, Stevie Wonder sang about us (women) as being "My Cheri Amour" (My Sweet Love), while another popular male group called us "Sunshine On A Cloudy Day". In the early 70's, women were not afraid to cry out "You're The One That I Want" along with Olivia Newton John, while we then openly confessed that we were "Hopelessly Devoted To You".

But by the mid 70's, Rick James among others redefined us as a "Super Freak" that was really super freaky. While in the background, men were yelling, "Give it to me, Baby"! Then Hall &

Oats opened up our realm of sexuality by calling us, "Man Eaters"! Of course, Parliament had already given us our measurements..."She's A Brick House". And that worked out well since our clothes were "Skin Tight". And while most of us were just "Stayin' Alive", another Anita was telling people that they could "Ring My Bell". And even though, people were asking "...are relationships possible?" Others were questioning, "How Deep Is Your Love" and an earlier Michael Jackson just wanted to "Dance With You", but Vanity was at the range with "Sex Shooter" and Prince was just starting to get busy with his new sex toy: "Darling Nikki". Although a revised Michael wasn't far behind with "Dirty Diana".

Next thing you know, Usher is talkin' about, "You Make Me Want To Leave The One I'm With And Start A New Relationship"; isn't that called premeditated cheating? But, women were no better. They would easily take another woman's no good man, because you got girlfriends telling their girlfriends, "Girl, Would You Still Want Him, If You Knew What I Know"....based on these apparently low standards for men, the answer would have to be "Yes!" She probably WOULD still want him! And if she got him, she wouldn't have to worry about knowing what to do with him because, Lil' Kim got a whole list of songs that will give you your step by step "I Wanna Sex You Up" directions.

If we didn't know it then, we know it now that the 80's and 90's led to an even playing field where both women and men could consider themselves equal players in The Mating Game. It's no wonder Snoop Doggy Dogg got pissed and reset the tone again claiming, "I Don't Love Them Hos No Mo'!" Let's keep it real, we all know there is little loyalty among women, when it comes to men. Or as Michelle N'degochello put it, "If That's Your Boyfriend, He Wasn't Last Night". But there is still a small handful of women singing you can "Get OUT". Hell, with all the drama, it's no wonder people's hearts are just plain "Frozen" as Madonna put it.

So, what's the answer? You can't stop playing the game, because the game is never over. So, what's the answer? Maybe the answer is to pick better. So let's look at...

The Screening Process
The Qualifiers.

Money, physical appearance, mental state, sexual preferences, availability and marital readiness are what we call the categories of qualifiers. What's important would be your preferences relative to those categories. Everyone has a list of preferences relative to the Qualifiers. These are the preferences that you would like to see in a person. You have certain standards that are mandatory and others that are just plain extra (the whipped cream on top of the sundae). The items that you rank as being most relevant and essential, are what I call the "Qualifiers."Your minimum standards are based on the decisions you make regarding what's acceptable and what's not under the "Qualifiers." These minimums help set what we call the "Standards". Your Standards and Qualifiers help answer certain questions, like:

1. How much money do you want him to have?

2. Do you want a man with muscles from head to toe or a slim and trim physique?

3. What kind of person must she be mentally?

4. What kind of sex must she enjoy?

5. Can he be married, divorced, a player or available, and (if you are interested in getting married) is he marriage material?

Do you see how it works? You are evaluating what is important before meeting a person. These minimums are mandatory. Therefore, if a guy satisfies the minimum Standards within the Qualifiers, then you will consider him for boyfriend material. Everything else is negotiable, but he must meet the minimum Standards within your Qualifiers. So, let's look at the first Qualifier.

Money. Money is an important element to everyone. However, to some, it's more important than to others.

I will never forget the time I was looking in Forbes Magazine, during the issue that had the 500 richest people in America. I'm always interested in that kind of information. So, I flipped the page to the list and started at the top. About the 5th person down, I saw an unfamiliar woman's name. Of course, I was very interested. It said that she had acquired several billions, within only 2 years! I was impressed and very curious to know how she did it. The final column on the line noted the industry or means in which the person noted made their fortune.

I looked to the final column of this woman's name and under method of acquiring money, she had listed "divorce"! I thought, "okay!" Girlfriend's just keeping it real. Hell, she doesn't have to play games with anybody, she got hers. Several billion, if I recall correctly. She got in the Mating Game and played to get paid, and DID!

However, not everyone requires a potential date to be a billionaire. Some women just want a professional man. Some men, just want a woman who is financially independent. But whatever it is that you want, you need to know, because it is most definitely one of the Qualifiers for screening.

Physical Appearance. Some men want a tall and slender woman. Some women want a man that is "cut" (muscular: a well built body)! To some women, their definition of physically attractive does not include his face, it's all about the BODY. It makes a difference. What's your idea of attractive?

Some women just want a pretty boy, whereas a well-built body that shows time at the gym is not required. It's important to know if you have a minimum standard or if you're flexible.

<u>Mental State.</u> There are men who don't like women with opinions. Whereas, there are women who love to be with a guy who can be mentally stimulating; so much so that he can be a fun opponent arguing (I mean... passionately discussing) topics of interest. Men can be similar, in this respect. Some men want a woman who can think and others want a woman who will cater.

A friend of mine went to the islands on a vacation. She was generally happy with her life and herself and this vacation was really a way of celebrating those joys in her life. Well, while she was on the island, she met an African-American man on vacation. Things went well and he invited her on a date that evening.

She was excited. She wore something nice, went on the date, discussed many things and truly enjoyed his conversation. He shared his opinions about various things and she shared hers. She hadn't had an opportunity to really talk to someone with such passionate views in a long while, so she was truly looking forward to seeing him again. Well, the next day he didn't call her. She really didn't know what was wrong. Slightly disappointed, she pushed herself to enjoy the rest of her vacation and returned home the following week.

Well, when she returned to the U.S., she told a close girlfriend what had happened with this guy. Her girlfriend happened to know this particular man and told her that this guy was a millionaire! Furthermore, she told her that it was well known that he was turned off by women who were mentally independent and thought for themselves.

Umm... Sad, but a true story.

Sexual Preferences. Men may not tell you this, but men (as well as women) all have a favorite sexual position. Sexual compatibility for a man entails that a woman can enjoy sex in the position that brings him the most joy.

I tell you this, ladies, because if a guy is trying to nudge you to have sex in a different position, he may be nudging you toward that most favored position (even though, he will not verbally tell you this). And there are some women that are pretty INFLEXIBLE, when it comes to trying new things. You really could be missing out by not trying something new. Who knows, it could become your favorite position too. However, if you try it and don't like it, then at least you can say, "I KNOW I don't like it like THAT!"

Availability. This is a difficult one because, guys who are playing around on a serious basis will take their wedding ring off. They know that women are looking. You CAN'T really trust them to tell you, because, ...Hell! If he's currently lying to his wife or girlfriend, he's already lying to you. And no one can really tell if he is in a relationship with a serious girlfriend, because those relationships come and go with the wind.

However, one pretty good way to tell if something funny is going on is if you ask for his phone number. If he GIVES you a pager number, he is either married, got several women, working a lot or always on the move.

If he REFUSES to give you his HOME phone number, then he's either homeless, married, living with a serious girlfriend, playing the field or all of the above.

If he GIVES you his HOME phone number and you call and he actually answers, the number could be a separate line in his house reserved for his extra marital affairs, a work number given to him by his company or he's okay. I know that was helpful and I'm glad I could be of service to provide you with this valuable information.

Marital Readiness. Some men just are NOT ready to get married. Just as, some women are NOT ready to tie the knot. Readiness for a serious relationship depends on what you ultimately want and where you are in your development.

Some people just don't feel that they are ready to have a serious relationship. However, the bottom line is until you are ready as a strong individual, you will not be ready to make a strong couple.

How Do Fools Fall In Love?

What is your method of falling into a relationship? I can think of four. Personally, I think falling into anything is a problem. I prefer to walk in with my eyes wide open and with the full intention of doing so, but to those of you who want them, here they are...

Friends to Lovers.

Some people like to find out more about a person and get to know who they are before they make the move to something more. The advantage of this is that you will know if you LIKE him (or her) before you LOVE him and you can find out what kind of person you are getting involved with. With this knowledge up front, you know if he is the kind of guy that loves them and leaves them or the kind of guy that is nice, sweet and tactful until the end. The person who moves from Friends to Lovers is not using sex for a quickie. They are looking for a meaningful relationship. It doesn't necessarily need to be a permanent move to lovers, but obviously the relationship is the focal point and the decision to make the move or not becomes an added or extra step to further your already existing relationship.

The possible negative side to becoming her friend first is that you could be labeled as a "nice guy" or a "friend" which for some guys is the kiss of death and more often than not means that they will not be considered for the position of boyfriend (or girlfriend). People who do this are either trying to tell you that they are not interested for reasons they don't want to say or are (quite possibly) at a less developed phase in their growth were they still want bad boys or naughty girls to play with. Either way, it's always easier for the rejected person to believe the later of the two explanations. It just goes down smoother.

Slow Burning Flame.

While some jump in, others like to take it one step at a time and look down the corridors before taking the next step. You never know what little surprises are waiting around the corner, or what skeletons might jump out of the closet. This is the slow and comfortable way of moving in. This method lessens the potential for regret, by not moving to fast too soon.

Reluctantly Yours.

If you have been hurt or are not sure about making that step, you will fall into this category. This is mainly done out of uncertainty or due to previous painful experiences. Moving in reluctantly is a matter of overcoming some previous personal complications or roadblocks. However, everything has its own time. A person who moves slower does so because he or she feels more comfortable with the pace or just doesn't want to make the journey. The challenge is in finding out which is so.

Lust to Love.
Lust does not equal love. Many people will say, "I saw her and I fell head over heals in love." No, that's not what happened. He saw her and he lusted (after) her. He then got lucky as she happened to be someone he could actually have feelings for, and those feelings developed into love. Lust is not love. Lust is appreciating someone's body. Love is appreciating someone's mind, body and soul. You cannot understand what a person's goals are from across the room. You cannot know a person's passions, ideas, or interests from across the room. You didn't find love. What you found was lust and you got lucky and lust then grew into love. However, not everyone is that lucky.

Kate met Kevin at a function. It was love at first sight (or so she said). Their first night together was hot and passionate. Over time their relationship began to grow. While they initially started out seeing each other once or twice every week, that then grew to two or three times. And after about 5 months, they just decided, "What the Hell; let's move in together."

So they did. The sex was great! Their time together was great and they were having fun and still enjoying their own lives. They had the best of both worlds.

Well, the unexpected happened and Kate had to have an operation, it was minor, but any operation appears major. However, in the course of her recovery, the doctor advised her not to have sex for three weeks in order to let the cuts heal.

Well, her first day home from the hospital, her boyfriend, Kevin, was great. He brought her breakfast in bed and flowers. He was extremely attentive. However, the second or third night, Kate noticed something, kind of odd. They didn't have anything to talk about. The sounds in the room were filled with the talk from the television and the voices from Kevin's tapes, but no discussion between the two of them.

When Kate, realized this, she immediately asked Kevin some basic questions, like...

"What's your favorite sport?"

He said, "Skiing".

The only problem with that was that Kate hated the cold. Then she asked Kevin, "If you could live anywhere in the world, where would you live?"

He said, "Alaska".

She thought, "Alaska!"

He explained that he loved nature and while it was extremely cold in the winter, it was extremely beautiful in the Spring when all the natural things bloomed.

Kate hated the country. She loved the city. "Oh my God!", she thought, "I can't believe I'm just now seeing this."

The only thing they had in common, was the great sex. Well, sex will do that to ya. And that's what happens sometimes, when you expect lust to grow into love

Lessons Women Could Learn from Men

While it's true that the differences between men and women create the on-going conflict. It is just as important to mention that men could learn by example from women and women could also learn by example from men. The first lesson being...

1. Women should learn how to masturbate...well.

I know there are women that are thinking right now, "I know she didn't write what I think she wrote." But yes, I did! Remember, I'm not writing this book to make friends. I'm writing it to tell you how it "tis". And what I'm telling you is that women should learn the lesson from men that it is advantageous to learn how to masturbate. Why? Because before a woman can tell a man how to turn her own, she first needs to acquire the road map for herself, so that she can provide the directions. Now, that may sound crude, but if you don't know how to reach orgasm, how can you expect a man to blindly do it for you?

That's why during sexual experiences, men are always going to get theirs (reach orgasm), because they've been working their own personal sex show solo for quite some time, long before they decided to add a partner. By the time they move up to the next level of actually having sex with a person, they know exactly how to reach the climax of their own show. It's women who are getting left out in the dark, thinking to themselves, "Damn, I could have had a V8!"

Secondly, masturbation is a great safe way to experience sexual fantasies. If you are thinking of a new potential experience, you can first play with the idea to see if it really works for you. It's safe from STDs because no actual contact takes place and it's safe from ridicule because no one knows about it but you. If the fantasy continues, then maybe you can consider taking it to the next level and actually doing it. And lastly, masturbating allows you to become adventurous and familiar with all the fun things available at the sex shop.

2. *Women should be more independent: emotionally and financially.*

Every man feels that it is mandatory for him to be independent in a variety of ways. Financially, he strives to always have a job, because the thought is that "a man should be able to support his family." Emotionally, he doesn't hesitate to detach himself from a relationship. While in contrast, there are women who find themselves grabbing the first man that comes along, just so she can have food on the table and few dollars to pay her bills. People prey on women like these that aren't financially or emotionally able to walk away. Therefore, women could learn the lesson of independence from men, and not allow themselves to be purchased at such a low bargain basement price.

3. Women should reclassify what we call a "relationship".

To men, having sex does not necessarily a relationship make. Whereas, women are too quick to define a moment of pleasure or a few common interests as a "relationship". Women move too quickly, only to discover that what they thought was a "relationship", was really just a friendship with a bit of casual sex.

4. Women should continue to value their female friendships, before, during and after marriage.

Men value their nights out with the boys. They continue to keep strong relationships with their male friends before, during and after a relationship with a woman. A man attempts to integrate his new woman or wife into his existing life. Women, instead decide to cut and remove parts of their life and replace it with him. As a result, she generally tends to feel challenged or threatened of her man's relationship with his boys.

Women make the mistake of devaluing their relationships with the girls, after he says, "I do." In a woman's mind, her husband and family become her world, but in a man's mind his world has not gotten smaller to exclude individuals, but has instead gotten bigger to include his wife and potentially a child. Women, exclude, while men include and that's the mistake that women make.

A female's relationship with the girls can help her continue to have a life outside of her married one. It can keep her vibrant and busy in the mix such that she can better appreciate her time together with her family.

5. Accept the gentleman's rule of "don't kiss and tell".

We've mentioned this element before under the aspect of Female Etiquette. However, it could be viewed as coming from the gentleman's rule. Women view a man who kisses and tells as childish and immature. In a similar way men can say the same for women who have had some bad experience with a man and then decided to tell the whole world. There is a time and a place for everything. Everybody doesn't need to hear about the intimate details of wrong doing that took place after sex. You are only hurting yourself when you indirectly tell a new guy that you're TOO trusting and you're TOO blind. So, take it from gentlemen and don't kiss and tell other men about YOUR shortcomings.

6. There is no time-line.

Women cannot help feeling rushed by all the factors that say she should be in a serious relationship by 23, married by 25 and with child before 28. While we all laugh at how a woman in the 1950's was considered an old maid, if she was not married by 23, and although we love to say that we've come a long way... [baby], the truth is we haven't come that far. For women the time-line has merely moved up a notch from 23 to 25. While women attempt to find anyone who will run them to the altar, men are content to wait it out for something they want or until they are sure. And while I say this is a lesson that women could learn from men, I also still see how difficult it is to resist the temptation of the forces that be to hurry up and get married, so you too can get divorced and live happily ever after.

Lessons Men Could Learn from Women

1. There is a level of gratification above sex.

Sex to a man is what marriage is to a woman. This is a sad reality that has been confirmed many times. Which is the belief that, if men didn't have to get married, they wouldn't. If men could have an unlimited amount of sex with their person of choice without marriage, they would. That's why I say, what men could learn from women is that there is a level above sex that can bring them a greater degree of fulfillment and joy. It comes from sharing something special with ONE woman. You're not just sharing sex, you are sharing your emotions, your feelings...your life. She becomes someone you can trust in the toughest of times and is the person who has got your back that will rush to bail you out when you go under. That's a true partner or a comrade in the game of life.

2. Communicating is better than guessing.

Talking is not communicating. Talking is one-way communication. Communication is when you listen and then you speak and then you listen again. Women communicate, some talk, but men hesitate to do either. Men would rather hold it in, not discuss it or try to figure it out. That's why men don't stop at the gas station for directions. They would rather be lost than communicate with someone and work it out. Communicating with the gas station attendant is similar to communicating with your girlfriend or wife. When you stop to ask for directions you usually find out that you're not exactly were you thought you were. And had you not stopped to check, you would have wasted a lot more time than you realized. By stopping and discussing the matter, you now know that every effort you make from this moment is focussed in the right direction. And, that is a lesson that men could learn from women.

3. Having sex is a choice.

There are men that are content to live in a primal mind set. By that I mean, they work on instinct. If a man sees a woman and finds her physically attractive, it's nothing for him to have sex with her within their first meeting. Why? "I saw her, I was attracted to her and wanted her." There are married men that still have that very same attitude about sex.

Men are more apt to give into a primal desire to have sex, whereas women, hesitate for a moment to consider what having sex with someone else might do to her life, her relationship, her marriage, her children, her emotional state and her income.

Men don't put that much thought into the matter. Not even when they have more to lose. If they did, you wouldn't have professional athletes going around the globe populating the world and then writing books with pride about how they slept with thousands of women. You would think that these men, of all men, would at least recognize the consequences of their choices relative to their INCOME. Fathering a child can be an expensive proposition for an NBA or NFL player. When you make millions, one roll in the hay could be the most expensive roll you've ever had, yet men of every income bracket (high and low) continue to father children outside of their permanent or intended relationships. At the very least, you'd think they'd choose to wear a condom, but they don't.

Sadly enough, men still choose to view sex as a primal act and not as a matter of choice in ever aspect, from maybe he will to maybe he won't. And this is a lesson that men could learn from women, that having sex is a choice that can indirectly or directly affect several other aspects of their life.

Of course, a book about mating wouldn't be complete without a section that answers the age old question of …

Why Don't Guys Call?

Imagine for a moment, you get dressed up and go out. You think you look hot. You see a guy, you give him your number. You finish enjoying the party and feel that it was worth your while because you met someone who might be special.

The next day comes, and no call. The day after that comes and still no call. You don't understand it. You met this guy. You had a really great time talking to him. You both laughed and you discovered you had a lot in common, so why didn't he call?

Was he just interested in doing a Bait & Tag? We sporadically selected five men at a conference, gave them the above scenario and asked them, "Why wouldn't you call the next day?" This is what they said:

1. "I changed my mind. I get a number from a girl and sometimes I just don't feel the same way about it the next day."

2. "Yes, we had a great conversation, but I don't know if I wanted to get involved in a real relationship and that's where that appeared to be heading."

3. "I got several numbers that night. I just called the ones that I thought would give me what I wanted. I just wanted to have a good time, maybe some good sex and that's it. This other girl wanted a relationship, and that wasn't my objective for the night. Yes, she was nice. Yes, we had things in common, but that was not what I was looking for. We had fun talking, but that was it. What do you want me to do, act hateful and just abruptly cut off conversations, just because I've decided she's not going to make my call back list?"

4. "I might have been out with my boys having a great time, and I just happened to meet someone nice, but I've already got a girlfriend. What am I going to tell her? Sorry, you seem nice, but I'm already in a relationship? I don't feel I need to go into all that detail. Not calling is easier. No explanation is necessary."

5. I was playing the numbers...

To those of you who don't understand what "playing the numbers" means, there are guys that need to BOOST their egos. These men have girlfriends, wives or whatever. They know that they're suppose to be in monogamous relationships, but they still feel the need to know that they COULD date other women, if they wanted to, right

NOW. So, they go out with the guys and approach women, only to get phone numbers, not because they plan on calling, but because their egos need to know that if it were all over tomorrow with their girlfriends, they could still approach other women, and those women would be interested. Playing the numbers is a game that men use to entertain themselves. It's not necessarily about quality, it's about quantity and the person with the most numbers collected, wins.

Why Don't Women Call?

We sporadically selected five women from the same conference and asked them the same question that we asked men about "why they don't call men back" and the answers were the same, but also included:

1. "I really didn't want his number when he gave it to me. I was just being nice by taking it."

2. "It seemed like a good idea at the time, but then when I called his house, some woman answered and that was the end of that number."

3. "It was a pager number, and I'm not trying to be played. If a man can't give me his home number, he's doing something he shouldn't be doing."

4. "I did call. I left one message on his voice mail. After that it was on him. When he didn't call back, that meant that the interest was not mutual. And I'm not about to chase after a man because I don't need to; I got Game!"

Breakup Methods

We've all experienced a breakup, a few of which we didn't even know were intended to be breakups. I remember watching an episode of LOVELINE on MTV, only to see a guy who was being completely ignored by his (so-called) girlfriend. The guy asked the show's hosts, "Do you think she's trying to tell me something?"

Hell, yes! I say. Not everybody likes to verbally come out with it and say, "I don't want to see you're ass anymore." Unfortunately, that leaves some people in limbo, not knowing or understanding that a breakup was intended. So, let's go through some of the breakup methods that men and women use.

Drift.
I call this first method the Drift, because that's what is intended to happen. A boyfriend stops calling; she says she forgot your phone number; he stops spending time with you. Why? Because the intention is to breakup through the process of avoiding you; hoping that you will just drift away. It is an implied breakup. The hope is that you will not

put up with it and quietly move on, but the unfortunate reality is that there are people who try to hang on and end up being the second, third or fourth girl in a harem of several women. He doesn't respect these women, nor does he care if they stay or go. They become disposable sex experiences and are purely kept for sexual use, like on permanent booty call.

In this method, he or she really doesn't want you around anymore. However, if you persist to stick around, despite all that is happening, you lose your credibility. You've indirectly proven that he/she can do and say anything and you will still be there. In the eyes of the other person, you've proven you will stick around no matter what! This is worse than if you had left, because now he knows he can do anything and you will still stick around. Contrary to what you believe at that moment in time, he doesn't care if you stay or go. So, he has nothing to lose by keeping you around now.

You, on the other hand, keep losing as time goes by. You've already lost his respect; you've become an instrument for sex... when he has no one else better. You continue to lose time, because you are wasting it waiting on him to change his mind. You're constantly missing out on guys who would treat you with respect and value, because you're sitting at home waiting for his call. This is a Lose-Lose Proposition for you. You lose all the way around. Whereas, he is in a Win-Win Position. He's dating other women that he likes. He's got you on the side as a stand by, you're not going anywhere, and he's got his freedom: Win-Win for him.

She's CRAZY!

I cannot tell you how many times I've seen this method used. When men are done with you, the best way to discredit you in the eyes of the new girlfriend is to say that you are out of touch with reality; you're a LIAR...you are out of control, or in short, "She's CRAZY!"

Now, I've had many girlfriends that this happened to, and I've known them all very well, so I can honestly tell you that none of them were really crazy. Upset maybe. Mad maybe. ENRAGED...maybe. Pissed off? Definitely.. But if she is all of these things, then she becomes the perfect candidate to be labeled as "crazy".

Why would a man call his old girlfriend crazy? Let me set the tone for you. A man's got a new girlfriend over at his apartment. He doesn't want her asking questions about the old girlfriend that keeps calling, yelling at him and then hanging up the phone. How is he going to explain that? Simple. "My old girlfriend is CRAZY!" The sad reality is that the new girlfriend buys that shit. Why? Because she wants to believe it.

To believe that the past girlfriend is NOT crazy would mean that her new boyfriend DID something to the old girlfriend to make her upset. This, of course, is something that new girlfriend doesn't want to consider because that would mean something is wrong with her man or that there is an error in her judgment of character by choosing this guy. Both of which mean that she has made a mistake and that in itself is a hard pill to swallow. Since she has not blatantly experienced a breach of trust in her guy, she assumes the "out of sight, out of mind" rule, meaning that she hasn't seen any problems with him so it must have been the old girlfriend who was out of her mind. Therefore the old girlfriend is CRAZY! You see how that works.

Now, in reality, what new girlfriend should be thinking is, "Umm, boyfriend didn't take care of his old business (conclude this relationship with the old girlfriend), before he started on his new business (dating ME)!" If the new girlfriend correctly thought about it like that, then she would start asking the right questions. That's when she would begin to realize that there is nothing wrong with his previous girlfriend. This is just his method of breaking up with women. This means that when he gets done with new girlfriend, guess who's going to become crazy next? You got it! You.

Guys tend to use the same breakup method over and over again. Once they find one that works, they become creatures of habit and repetition. As soon as he is done with you, and finds someone new, the quick method of getting rid of you will be to call you crazy, too.

Up Front.
While people claim to wish people were up front and honest with them AFTER another method has been used, the truth is some people just can't handle it initially. Why? For some people, breaking-up requires them to be hardcore, mean, cold, crass, assholes. But being Up Front doesn't require being a shit-head about it. Whether you want to admit it or not, most situations would be better off, if people just came out with the truth Up Front.

I've met a couple of women who have gotten married, only to finally come out later that they were gay. Talk about a painful pill to swallow, man or woman. And these men were hurt; they loved these women. Instead of being Up Front and telling these men in the beginning, they waited two kids and a dog later to spring it on them. Of course, one or two of those women will tell you that they didn't discover it until later in life, although I would suspect that they just chose later in life to be Up Front.

I've met people who have walked down the aisle KNOWING that they did NOT love someone only to go through with it and hurt the person they said they loved five years later, after they had built a life together. The Up Front Method could be equated to taking the brunt of a hurt pill all at once instead of little by little over time with compounded crazy high interest later, as is done with the Drift.

All in all, if you can handle it, the Up Front Method with tact is the better of the ways to go.

Chapter

❷

This Is How We Do It!

■ ■ ■

Good Sex!
*"It's more than an act of pleasure.
It's a state of mind."*

Sex is a tool in The Mating Game that is better globally defined as the act of pushing the right buttons to cause an individual to reach a heightened form of pleasure. Intercourse is just one way of doing that.

Sex...? Yes, it's sex! ...By the revised definition. So, in the true essence of the word "sex", intercourse is optional. Understanding this, you may also now see how sex can be a tool.

Sex, the Secret Weapon!

It's the perfect instrument to blind and manipulate men and women of every kind, in the realm of The Mating Game. The power in sex, is that it can mean, be or represent a wide variety of things. However, like many things, the advantage of sex can also be perceived as its disadvantage. That is...sex seems to never quite mean the same one thing to any two people.

The trick, in using sex as a weapon successfully, is in reading the person. Figuring out what a person wants and then using sex to fulfill that feeling, desire or need. This is what we're talking about. The biggest problem, however, with using sex as a tool to your own personal advantage is that it can quickly be turned into a weapon targeted toward your own personal demise.

So, What Kind of Sex Are You Having?

Why do men and women get hurt? It's typically because they have sex NOW, and THEN start to ask certain questions about the kind of sex they just had LATER.

I was watching a television show one evening and saw Dr. Gray (the author of "Men are from Mars, Women are from Venus"). Well, I couldn't help but notice that what he was saying about sex being divided into categories was true! It made sense; however I didn't agree with his definition of the first 3 levels. So, I decided to include my altered version of his theory in this chapter.

According to Dr. Gray, there are four levels of sex:
1. Casual Sex
2. Intimate Sex
3. Monogamous Sex
4. Spiritual Sex

Let's take a look at my definitions of these levels.

Casual Sex
This represents the first level of the sexual experience. It's used to fulfill the most basic of needs: pure sexual desire or lust! On this level, sexual gratification and immediate fulfillment are the recurring goals. Under this heading, there are two main types of Casual Sex: One-Night-Stand Sex and Romantic Sex.

One-Night-Stand Sex is that one-night sexual encounter experienced when you meet a guy, take him home, sleep on it and wake up the next day with fond memories, but no guy. There's no attachment, no commitment, and once it's over, it's over. A special item to note here is that you CAN have several One-Night-Stand Sex sessions with the same person, but each time the session is over, you're done. It's very detached and used purely to service a sexual need, desire or purpose. Bill Bellemy brought it to everyone's attention several years ago when he nicknamed this type of sex the "Booty Call".

Men, be careful. Whether you know it or not, just as you rate women on their potential prospect for "girlfriend" status, women do the same with men. If you don't meet a woman's basic standards (within her Qualifiers), you could be placed on, what I call "*Permanent Booty Call Duty*". That means that you are only good for One-Night-Stand Sex. That is of course when she can't find anyone else. You are a second choice, a stand by, or a back-up. In her eyes, you are not acceptable boyfriend material. You're a sex machine. Now, I'm sure there are some guys who are okay with that. In fact, there are even some men thinking right now... "hmmm... How can I apply for that Permanent Booty Call position?"

...But men, it's not something you can actually apply for. It's more of a default status that you acquire after you fail every other possible use, but one. Can he hold a good conversation? No. Does he have a good shoulder to cry on? No. Hmmm... but he's GREAT in BED. Ah,

"Permanent Booty Call Duty!" However, not everyone ventures out to have Booty Call Sex.

Have you ever wondered why women have that, "I will NOT sleep with him on the first date" rule? It's a safeguard against this kind of sex! Women of every age don't know why they're suppose to follow this rule, but obviously somewhere along the line, a woman realized that her chance of avoiding One-Night-Stand Sex was greatly improved, if she completely avoided sex on the first night all together. That information, was eventually passed on in the form of this rule. And it's true, ladies. Men don't respect women that go down on the first date or encounter. It's like Monica sings, "I want to get down, but not the first NIGHT!" So ...don't!

In his mind, when a female has wild and kinky sex on their first date, he's NOT thinking, "What a GREAT woman! I can't wait to take her home to meet my family." He's thinking, "What a FREAK!! I just met this woman 30 minutes ago and now she's got my shit in her mouth! Is she this easy with everybody? Oh, I want to see her again... I definitely will, put this one on Permanent Booty Call Duty." (Smile.)

<u>Romantic Sex</u> is only a half step above One-Night-Stand Sex. It's the kind of sex that women dream of and read about in romance novels. Then go off on vacation to some tropical island and experience. She and he spend the weekend making

mad, passionate, romantic sex on the beach and then after they leave, the only thing left are beautiful memories. Unlike Stella and her grove, you both never see each other again, or at least it was never part of the bargain, nor was it a mandatory element of the deal. However, just as you can have several One-Night-Stand Sex sessions, you can also have several Romantic Sex sessions. He calls you to go away for the weekend. She calls him to meet her for an intimate dinner at her house. It's not really a relationship. It's just Casual Sex for an extended period of time (i.e.: a weekend fling) and a little more thought, planning and effort put into it; but it's still casual and detached.

Secret Sex. Now, under the heading of Casual Sex, there is also a thing called, Secret Sex. This type of sex was featured once on the HBO show "Sex in the City"; I really LIKE that series! This is the sex you have when the person involved is great at sex, but bad in most every other way that matters. Unlike a person on Permanent Booty Call Duty, this person actually has some positive features or characteristics, but those pluses represent only a small fractional push forward in their overall score. Unfortunately, their negatives outweigh their positive features and they end up being a small piece of the complete package required to pursue a real full-fledged relationship with.

So, instead of introducing this person to your friends and making them a part of your world, you keep him/her separate and apart from anything or anyone who is an important part of you. You do this because you are concerned about what your friends, associates and family might say or think. She or he does not fit your complete ideal of what a person YOU should be with should look, act or be like. ...but you still enjoy the sex a lot! So, you keep him/her off to the side. This distancing also makes them easy to dispose of later.

Blackout Sex. Another type of Casual Sex, is Blackout Sex. I think you're all familiar with this special genre of sex. Blackout Sex is, in fact, the sex you have but can't remember having the next morning. It's the sex you HAD with a co-worker at the company Christmas Party when you also HAD too many free shots of Bourbon. Blackout Sex is the sex you have and upon awaking the next morning are introduced to the person lying next to you in bed, on the floor, in the truck ...or wherever the wretched event took place. Now, it's ...not that you weren't introduced to your Blackout Sex partner last night, it's just that this is the first time you actually remember hearing their name.

Blackout Sex is sex under the influence (of alcohol or drugs) and is therefore, unfortunately, the most dangerous kind of sex, because it's usually done without a clear head and that means, more often than not, unprotected sex. You usually regret or just want to plain forget Blackout Sex, the morning after, because it can impact you negatively with:
- unkind gossip at the office,

- a STD (Sexually Transmitted Disease), or
- phone calls or personal visits from someone you wish didn't have either your phone number or your address...let alone your name.

Intimate Sex

This is the next step up. Intimate Sex marks the point when you begin to connect with someone and your sexual experience with that person begins to distinguish itself as more than an act of pleasure, it's special, unique or irreplaceable. Now, I did NOT say that a person who admits to experiencing Intimate Sex only has sex with that ONE person. No. That's not what I said. I said that person admits to experiencing sex on a higher plane with ONE person. Now, that individual may still have Casual Sex with other people; in fact, they probably are. However, this person has hit the middle ground in between Casual Sex and Monogamous Sex and is beginning to realize or discover that sex with one person can be something more than a basic instinct.

Monogamous Sex

Monogamous Sex is an attempt to move up to the next level of intimacy. It is to allow sex to bring a couple closer together through feelings and emotions. These are, of course, the serious dating relationships or the married couples. This is the act of using sex to commit, grow and develop together.

Spiritual Sex

Spiritual Sex is something that we aspire to through Monogamous Sex. It is the act of consolidating both love and sex to become a part of something much bigger. It allows two people to bond on a special level of intimacy that could only be defined as spiritual. You both begin to become so familiar with each that each might refer to the other as a soul mate.

So, with all of this in mind, what do I expect you to do with all of this new found information? Recognize the type of sexual invitation you are being offered BEFORE you accept it, not AFTER!

- *Situation Number 1:* If you meet a guy in a club and he invites you back to his place for some fun? Know that he's not interested in starting a relationship! You are about to have One-Night-Stand Sex! So, recognize it! No agreements have been made and no promises of tomorrow are being extended. If you decide to accept the terms and conditions of this agreement and have One-Night-Stand Sex, don't cry tomorrow when he doesn't call. And even if he does call, realizing that his call was not part of the initial bargain up front, makes the call a plus instead of a painful reality in the end, if he doesn't.

- *Situation Number 2:* If you start seeing a guy, the two of you go out a couple of times and the day after you have sex, he doesn't call you anymore? You just had Romantic Sex. Recognize it and move on!

- *Situation Number 3:* If you are at a Christmas Party and a very attractive, drunk guy propositions you for sex. He's trying to have Blackout Sex! Tomorrow you will be his biggest regret! So, unless you are just plain desperate, walk away! This man is indirectly saying to you through his proposition, "The only way I would have sex with you is if I was DRUNK! ...and I am, so, let's DO this!" Recognize this for the INSULT it is and just say, "NO!"

- *Situation Number 4:* If you are constantly dating a woman who will not take you to meet any of her friends and she doesn't want to go to your favorite spots, you are a Secret Sex partner! Either except the terms of the sex without commitment, or walk away, but do NOT ask this woman to marry you! It would be a rude awakening.

So, use your new found information "for the purpose of good, not evil" when making decisions, such that you may make them with your "eyes WIDE open" (instead of your eyes WIDE shut: hint, hint...the movie). Then, maybe you won't be so disappointed by the outcome later.

So, Where Are You?

We've talked about sex, now let's talk about relationships. In the course of interviewing a variety of people, it's my opinion that there are generally five phases in the development of a relationship:

1. The Hunt
2. Discovery
3. Friendship
4. Intimacy
5. Comfort

The Hunt.

This is the first phase. Most people fall in love with this phase, so much so, that they never want to leave it. These are the people who only stay until the chase is complete. After he's got you, he's ready to move on to the next person, victim or prey. I refer to these people as the "Gigolo Vampires". Be careful of these people or they could steal all of your life's blood: your vibrance, your carefree attitude, your joy of life and your vitality.

People that are caught in the phase of The Hunt are the ones that the silly Mating Game rules were made for. You only call once for every three times that they call or you pretend that you don't like them, when, in fact, you believe he is absolutely FINE (extremely attractive)!!

Without a doubt, I cannot lie, The Hunt can be fun! It makes you feel attractive, desired and wanted. It gives you that false sense of being in control, when there's nothing "in control" about it. Regardless of what we may want to do, a person who is not ready to leave this phase, will NOT, until he or she is ready to do so. Individuals that go after people who are stuck in this phase eventually get hurt, because you both are playing the Mating Game. She wants the fun of The Hunt and he wants to move toward higher phases within a relationship. Pain is destined to enter into the picture. The two of you don't share the same goal.

Discovery.
Next, is the phase of learning about each other called Discovery. People stuck in this phase are somewhat amusing. I can't tell you how many men have openly complained about not being able to understand a woman. Then as soon as he feels he knows her, he's ready to leave. Why? Because, "She's not interesting anymore," ...so they say. These are the people caught in the phase of Discovery. They enjoy the intrigue and the mystery of discovering new secrets and elements of fascination about their new love interest. However, once the mystery is gone, so is she.

However, there are still those who use the Discovery Phase as a preliminary step toward a higher form of relationship. The problem is, of course, that you don't know which way a person will go once they get closer and uncover some of your secrets. It's a toss up. But if you knew the outcome in advance, it wouldn't be a Game, then would it...?

Friendship.

Friendship is the next step up in the development and growth of relationships. This phase marks the point at which two people begin to accept one another for who they are and for what they contribute to each other's lives: an ear to talk to, a positive word or two for encouragement, a shoulder to lean on, moments to share together, etc. This phase also marks reaching an initial stage of stability.

However, some relationships start as friendships. If two friends begin dating, they can either move back down toward "The Hunt" or move upward a notch toward "Comfort".

Intimacy

Intimacy is the battlefield in which many relationships are either won or lost. It's the middle ground between Friendship and Comfort, and is the time when friendships are either converted to the final phase or damaged because they couldn't make the middle passage.

Intimacy is also the time when couples decide to live together for a trial period, and represents the "Big Test" that many hesitate to take, for fear they may not pass (onto the next level of Comfort), but will instead pass onto the imminent death (of their relationship).

Comfort.
Comfort is the final phase that we all aspire to, dream of, make every effort and sacrifice to obtain, but upon reaching...dread. Comfort can be the kiss of death or the final stage before reaching 2.5 kids, a house, one picket fence and a dog later. Oddly enough, while we all strive to reach this phase of Comfort with that special someone, we also become easily bored with the same comfort that we so eagerly sought to achieve. That's why under Comfort, it's often recommended that we all periodically introduce new elements into the game (relationship) that would more closely be associated with earlier phases like The Hunt or Discovery. Going temporarily backwards allows or enables both to share new and exciting events, like the excitement of being asked out on a date by your husband (The Hunt) or the sweet sensation of getting a call to talk about nothing in the middle of the day with your girlfriend (Friendship).

Two reasons for occasionally introducing elements of lower phases include that every woman wants to feel desired and every man loves to unravel a new layer of intrigue about his wife or girlfriend. And elements of Discovery and The Hunt can do that. This is in part a way of reinventing or breathing new life into your Comfort zone (i.e.: relationship)

In addition to intrigue, very few people stop growing. We all continue to change and develop; therefore, it would only seem logical that these new elements would also be introduced into our Comfort zone (relationship). The hope is that by doing so, both individuals continue to contribute and grow together.

So, Why Do People Cheat?

Some would say, they cheat because they can; or because it's not sexually natural to be with only one person for life. However, it would appear that:
- some revel in the basic sexual pleasure;
- some enjoy the sexual variety of having more than one person at their beck and call, and
- some crave the joy of The Hunt and, the newness of a relationship.

These same people will tell you that learning about each other can be a seductive adventure. However, still a smaller group will confess to using cheating as a breakup technique. (They don't want a relationship and cheating offers a simple "no ask, no tell" leave policy.)

Despite a variety of explanations, the overall consuming reason appears to be the same. People cheat or become involved in another relationship because the new person in the picture brought something extra that was missing in the person's life.

Ask and answer honestly each of the following questions, assuming they were happening to you.

1. 👄 If you are a 50-year old man and an attractive woman approaches you, how do you think you would feel?

2. 👄 If you are a woman able to tell a man your deepest sexual desires and fantasies, and be given the opportunity to act upon them, how do you think that would make you feel?

3. 👄 If you are a man and able to leave the worries of the world behind and go to a hotel knock boots with an attractive woman, how would you feel?

The answer to all of these questions would be the same: "You feel *Great!!*" However, it doesn't always have to be that someone else can creep into your party and take your special someone. Don't forget that after you enter the phase of Intimacy or Comfort, you are still playing the Mating Game. It doesn't end after marriage or after he moves in. It's an ongoing series of moves and counter moves.

So, what can you do to never be cheated on again? Nothing. As an individual, you only have a 50% say in whether the relationship will continue or end. The other 50% belongs to the other person in it. And it is for that reason that sometimes despite what you may do or what he (she) may say or promise that there is no way to stop a cheating dog.

Why Are Most Men Dogs?

Are most men dogs? Or, are all dogs just other forms of men? You, tell me. There's got to be a more substantial reason why dogs are man's best friend and why men refer to their good friends as "their dogs." Whether the connection is definite or acquired, one can't deny that there is something going on with the similarity. Maybe it's how men operate, in the most primitive and animalistic of characteristics! However, one thing is most certain, men operate differently relative to women. And when it comes to relationships, the difference multiplies exponentially.

Men are basic and primal in their approach to life, to problems and to relationships. Women, on the other hand, tend to take the higher ground engaging first in thought, then consulting a game plan prior to execution. Compared to women, men just do and respond. Now, with respect to the thinking process, men do think! It's just with a different head. Men start the thought process with their little head (genitals) then work their way up toward their big head (brain). Women, however, start from the other end.

Now, despite how poor a woman's decision may be, every woman's sexual choice (sexual activity) was preceded by thought. This is not to say that a woman was not mislead into an act. A woman's information may have been incorrect or her vision short-sighted. However, make no mistake about it; if she did it willingly, she put some thought into it.

A woman's thought process starts at the brain (to look at long- or short-term advantages), moves down toward the heart (for logical long-term connections), and then continues down toward the genitals (for short-term satisfaction) to put the plan into action through sex.

Now because men consult with their little head first, their thought process is dominated by a basic need to have sex, before anything else. They are lustfully attracted to women, before the prospect of marriage or relationship ever enters the picture as a thought. A long-term relationship for them, doesn't start out as a relationship, it starts as a sexual or lustful encounter. There is little love, emotion or feeling attached to a man's decision. The entire process is very much a primal concept or basic instinct.

Now in the course of having sex to enact her plan, a woman strives to achieve both her perceived short-term and long-term goals (as previously calculated by the heart and the brain), she tends to develop emotions. While men are still shielded by ignorance; they haven't given a full effort of uncompromised thought (brain power) to it. This is still a one-man show (little head dictatorship). But because women tend not to give up the "coochie" (a loose term for the female sex part) without receiving confirmation that he has similar feelings to the same degree and level, he lies so she will put out (have sex). And this is why many women get hurt in the end. This is also why right after a breakup you hear women confess and complain about how he said, he loved her and would spend the rest of his life with her. When the truth is, immediately after some form of Casual Sex, he left never to be heard from again.

Men don't have feelings of their heart or emotional ties when they have sex...not in the beginning, anyway. That's why men are quick to say, "Well, I only slept with her ONE TIME!" You see, to a man, one-time sex (Casual Sex) does NOT a relationship make; sex one time is just SEX! Conversely, women get upset with this type of disregard by men because women view the act of sex (at all), regardless of the number of times, as being part of a relationship and it's growth. So, if we know this, why do men continue to do it and why do women continue to get upset about it? Because, regardless of the number of times it happens, women in these situations continue to BELIEVE that their relationship is at a higher phase of development than it actually is, while men continue to allow women to believe it. So while she's saving herself for him, telling every other interested man "no", he still feels free to have Casual Sex with every other interested women.

I had the fabulous experience of interviewing Theodore Whitcher, the writer and director of the movie "Love Jones" (I LOVED that movie!!). And one of the things I asked him about in his movie was: "Why did the male lead character in the movie feel no remorse when he appeared to lie about having a relationship with the OTHER woman that he had had sex with?" Theodore said: "Because [to a man] what he had with the OTHER woman was not a relationship; it was just sex." I rest my case. Or should I say: "WHOOP!! There it is!"

This is not to say that a man can't have a relationship. It's just that his process is different. For instance, if a man has experienced pain before in playing the game (i.e.: during dating or in a relationship) or he has experienced hurt when he attempted to get closer to a woman, then those feelings may resurface and impact his decision to remain in a new relationship. As a result, he may either stop the progression of the game (the relationship) or stop that game all together. It's those experiences that may stop him from moving forward and leave him in the world of Casual Sex. However, not everything is an event that we can stop.

If He's Gonna Do It, He's Gonna Do it!

Despite the common belief, cheating is not a guaranteed thing you can avoid. Women want to believe that it is. However, my belief is that the ultimate responsibility rests with the person doing the cheating. If they are not happy, or there is something they need to talk about, then it is that person's (who is considering cheating) responsibility to tell you that a problem exists BEFORE bringing someone new into the game. However, sometimes there's no problem to speak of.

Do you remember that movie *Fatal Attraction*? Well, if you can reflect back to recall the wife, you will remember that she appeared perfect, in every way that we would think of as being important. She was beautiful; she was loving; she was attentive; she was caring. So, why the Hell did the lead character, Michael Douglas, have an affair with Glenn Close? Two reasons, because he COULD, and because he WANTED to.

To a woman, neither reason is justifiable and yet, these are times when they are the very reasons that we're left to deal with. I'm sure there are still those of you who think it is all about looks or one's sexual ability! Well, Pamela Lee Anderson and the once Halle Berry-Justice would disagree with you.

Pamela and Halle Berry's looks are adored by millions of men. Yet, it did not stop Halle's ex-husband, David Justice, from looking at the candy in the flirtatious candy store of female options placed before him on a daily basis, nor did it stop Pamela's husband, Tommy Lee from continuing to openly have his way with many women publicly. In fact, the one woman who openly admitted to "playing around" with Pamela's husband, had many of the same characteristics as Pamela. This woman was blonde, dressed in a very revealing manner and appeared to be adventurous and out-going, just like Pamela. This only helps to prove one of my many points. The first being that men, ironically enough, most often, will go after mistresses that look almost identical to their wives or girlfriends. That kind of makes sense. Men, as women, are attracted to a favorite set of physical characteristics (i.e.: brown hair, brown eyes, etc.). Therefore, naturally that guy would be attracted to those same characteristics in another woman (unless, he's searching for physical variety). And against popular belief, it is not unusual for a mistress or the other woman to be considered less attractive, in the eyes of the female she is replacing or for whom she is a temporary substitute for.

However, the option of variety is true also. There are men who like variety and there idea of attractive is every type of body or flavor in the candy store. He will not be happy until he has had at least one of every kind of candy in the store. Women may ask, "What is the attractive feature then?" or "What does SHE have that I haven't got?" The answer is "different coochie." Therefore, physical beauty is NOT the exclusive or determining factor in a man or woman's decision to play around.

So, what will stop a man (or a woman for that matter) from cheating? If you're married, it would be his belief in his wedding vows. If you're in a serious relationship, it would be her commitment to making it work. Therefore, if he or she doesn't believe in either, there is nothing stopping him or her. And if that is the case, I have to ask, "Why are you with this person?"

Despite the fact that the cheater is ultimately responsible for his/her cheating, there is still a little footnote in the Mating Game referred to as the "Buyer's Beware". This means even though a guy (or a woman) may be cheating and as Whitney Houston put it in one of her songs, "...it's not right, but it's okay," women and men a like have to unfortunately be on guard to protect themselves from the people who have decided to do wrong and make them an accomplice to their wrongdoing (cheating).

How Can You Tell When a Guy is Still Playing the Field?

Note to the Reader: In this section, I use the pronoun, "He" but we all know it could be a "She" doing the cheating. So, read this, with the understanding that the "guy" could be a "gal".

So, watch out if...

1. *He's got a pager.*
You can't call him at home. You can't call him at work. So, how do you reach him? Call his pager. He's got to be living some where? Right? So, are you trying to tell me that he doesn't have a phone? Bull shit! If he can't give you his home phone number, then my advice would be, don't give

him yours. He is hiding something and I think we both know what it is: a girlfriend or a wife.

2. *He's got a voice mailbox; he never personally answers the phone.*

Guys have gotten smarter and technology has provided them with the options. He can give you what you think is his home phone number, but it is actually a voice mailbox. It sounds like a phone, but it's not. Most people connect their home phones to a voice mailbox, but not every voice mailbox is connected to a phone. You can purchase them much like a pager and leave it out in telephone cyberspace, safe from unsuspecting hands and available anywhere by phone. How can you tell if it's a voice mailbox? It's hard to tell, but one sure-fire guess is, if he never picks up the phone, then he's probably given you his voice mailbox. It's kind of an odd thing when you never seem to reach him. If that is the case, he's not just busy, he's busy playing the Mating Game with others and just plain "playing" you.

3. *He will not let you listen to his messages on the answering machine.*

If you have a comfortable relationship, then you have no secrets. Right? Well, if you can't listen to his phone messages, he's got secrets. He wouldn't care if you heard his Mom call. He wouldn't care if you heard his job call. So, what would make him upset? If you heard his other woman on an answering machine, you got it! Other women calling? Yes, that too.

4. He will not answer the phone, when you're there.

What's the big deal with picking up a phone? Who's calling? The electric company, your employer...again why would he NOT pickup the phone? Obviously, he doesn't want you to hear something. I could understand if he did it to avoid one call on a certain day. Everybody has those days, but EVERY time, every day! No. Something's going on and it doesn't look good.

5. The two of you start spending less time at his place and more time at yours.

After a while, it becomes more difficult to control people when they've been to his apartment for sex. They know where he lives and have a phone number. People can become aggressive and possessive. The best way to avoid another person from knocking on the door or constantly calling until someone picks up is to simply, go somewhere else, like her place. Her place is safe. You don't have to worry about the phone. You don't have to worry about unexpected visits. Her place puts her on guard, if nothing else and when he's done, he can go back to his place and put in for another Booty Call.

6. Sex is less frequent.

Despite what guys will tell you, they can't do it all night long. Most guys know how many rounds their good for in bed or in an evening. If he can only go four rounds and someone else got those four rounds, you aren't getting any. Do you see how it works. So, if he's giving someone else your four rounds, he won't be seeing you for a while. Or, if you know that he goes four rounds and you only got two, then you know someone else got your other two. This is what I mean by sex becomes less frequent.

7. He becomes disorganized and unable to plan ahead or keep commitments.

Cheating requires a lot of time. If you think about how difficult it is to plan one life, imagine how difficult it would be to plan four or six lives. A man or woman that cheats is living multiple lives: one life with each person he or she proclaims to have. If you think about it in that context, then you can see why it would become difficult for him or her to plan for events. Women sporadically stop by unannounced; one night with one woman turns into two nights. The cheater has to constantly accommodate changes to his/her schedule. When you accommodate one person, you have to cancel with another, so time becomes tight and appears to be disorganized.

8. He starts getting cheap about dates with you.

Cheating is expensive. Taking four men or women out to eat every week can add up. Therefore, the cheater, starts to get cheap. He simply can't afford the cost of up-keep. If you started out going to nice places and all of a sudden you are hitting McDonalds and he is asking you to cook, something is wrong. Now, I'm not talking about mixing it up a bit such that you spend a few evenings cooking at your house. I'm talking about night and day changes. If you DID get flowers, he can't afford them any more. If you USE to go out to eat, he only calls you after dinner. Things like that, very noticeable changes.

9. *Explanations about his time, become complex.*

A cheater needs to have some way of blocking time for other women. The way to best do that is to create some explanation that takes precedence over his time, so that you won't call him during his date with another person. Like:

"Are we going out tonight?"

"No, no. I've got to work tonight."

"Didn't you work late, last night?"

"Yes, yes, but I'm working on a big project."

"Well, how about if I bring you a picnic dinner over to the office?"

"No, no. That wouldn't be a good idea."

"Why?"

"I've got people working with me and, I don't know if it would be appropriate with you coming over. I mean it's after business hours. I'd have to clear it with building security...."

"Well, why would security mind?"

"Well, they just instituted this new POLICY, yes...they instituted a new policy restricting people in the building after hours, who are unauthorized personnel."

"Well, can I call you at work?"

"No, that wouldn't be a good idea. I mean I'm going to be deep into thought on these plans, it's going to be grueling."

See, he doesn't want her to call and he doesn't want her to come by because he's not going to be there! Building security could tell her that he never signed in or they could call up to his office and see that he's not answering his phone. But she can't tell him that he can't work late. So, it's a guaranteed out for the evening.

10. He doesn't call as frequently anymore.
Again, cheating requires time. With less of it, you don't have time to call as much as you use to. And if you did, she might want to see you. So, you're better off not calling as much.

11. He doesn't take you to his favorite places.
To take you to his favorite places, could mean getting caught by other women he's dating and previously taken to these places. Or be seen by his friends, who could inadvertently slip up and mention someone else they saw your guy with last week.

12. You never meet any of his friends or family.

Women that aren't introduced to family or friends, are not taken seriously. He doesn't accept you to be a long-term part of his life, so it's not necessary to introduce you to the other important people in his life. It's a bad sign, especially if you've been dating for many months and he has never once mentioned taking you to a family function. Families do have get-togethers, and family events. He's taking someone, it's just not you.

13. He doesn't talk to you about the intimate details of his life.

Guys that don't expect you to be around for the long haul are not going to open up and share their life with you. They will not talk about life's pressures and they will not include you in it. The thought is, "Why waste time, she'll be gone soon anyway."

14. You don't go out with him on Friday or Saturday nights.

Now some guys will disagree with me. There are a couple of men that said they love to go out on any other nights but those, because clubs are too congested to have fun. But, guys either reserve these two nights for the guys or they want to leave them open for someone more interesting that might come along between now and Saturday. If he tells you that he won't take you out on those two nights, he's either preparing to find someone else or you're not the one. Either way, it's bad.

How Does A Woman Snare A Man, ...Or Another Woman's Man?

Now, notice the title is NOT, "How Does a Woman Snare A GOOD Man". What I am about to tell you is NOT about snaring a man of quality. This is purely a matter of explaining a process. We will deal with the quality issue later.

Now, don't be misled by the title; men can use these steps too.

So, before another woman can move into assume your position, there are certain steps that she must exercise and that's what we're going to break down and explain: step by step.

Step one of the seduction:

The "Look"

The "Look" is the ability to stare directly into a man's eyes and make him feel that all he's said is interesting and fascinating. Sounds like I'm full of it, doesn't it? But, it's true.

It is easy to do. Yet the feeling that comes from merely a look is surprisingly effective. If you are unfamiliar with this method, here are a few of the steps to get you started:

1. Eye Contact

This is the first item of business. You must look directly into his/her eyes with a relaxed intensity that is more a reflection of active listening. Don't forget to throw in some natural eyebrow action.

2. Facial Expression

Don't look as though you're in pain or as if you have no idea what he/she is talking about. Look interested and comfortable with being there. Obviously your facial expression will change with the intensity of the subject matter. If the subject is extremely serious, you are going to show concern. If the discussion is light-hearted, naturally you're NOT going to look terrified. Ride the conversation like a wave. It's an adventure, and how you react to the discussion can be just as important, if not more, than your actual verbal interaction

3. Move Into Their Personal Space

Everyone has a comfort zone of space that's usually referred to as "personal space": 2 to 3 feet around a person. When an individual allows less than 3 feet in between the two of you, then you are considered to be in each other's personal space. This indirectly implies that you're getting "personal" with each other. It's a body language "thang". However, when you're in this space and the individual feels comfortable with you being there, this is considered to be intimate. Also, don't be afraid to touch during the conversation. Some common gestures might include just briefly brushing an arm or nudging someone to emphasize a joke. Of course, touching the face or hands would be something reserved for close friends. However, touching can also be a nice way to leave a conversation. As you say good-bye, simply touch him/her as you move away.

4. Never Allow Your Eyes to Roam

Can you recall talking to an attractive man, thinking that he was completely engrossed in your conversation, only to have his eyes swayed for a moment by the simple passing of a pretty woman? How did that make you feel? Even if it was for a moment, that brief moment said something. If it's true what they say, you know, "Actions speak louder than words," then that simple act was SCREAMING the thought: "I'm not sure I want to be spending time with you, especially if someone better is available. Because, I CAN be easily swayed from... you".

Yes or no? Tell me, I'm wrong. You can't; because, I'm not. It's true. Now think, if you picked up on that simple act, it would be obvious to believe that men are just as sensitive to a woman's head turning to see another attractive man in passing, also. So, what am I trying to say? Simply put, do the reverse of the Nike advertisement and "just ...Don't do it!"

The Lure

You've got his attention, now you lure him in with his own information. But how do you start the conversation? Simple, all you need is a beginning topic. And how do you get that? It all depends on where you are. If you're at a club, you might make a comment about the music. If you're at a professional event, you might strike up a conversation based on a seminar or the keynote speaker's speech and then roll over to an item of concern to the industry you both represent. If you are at the theater, you might make a comment about the play, or the quality of the performance. The days of "You look familiar," and "Have we met before?" were over five seconds after they were first used, and best left unused, unless they are actually true.

Once he/she starts talking, the rest is easy. All you need to do is listen and continue to sporadically make comments related to new information. Information that he or she will so graciously provide you with through the course of the conversation. Simple, right? It really is.

Flattery Will Get You Everywhere!

If people can be lured by conversation, then "flattery" is the tool used to activate the trap! Men, and women alike, love for others to glorify their accomplishments. (Wouldn't you?) I know that this is probably the point in the conversation where the people who are in more serious levels within the game (relationships) begin to think: "Now, why the Hell would I do that? Wouldn't he get tired of hearing the same admiration for a previous success over and over?"

I think the Mayflower Madam answered that question best with, "As a woman, do you ever get tired of hearing how pretty you are, how attractive you are, how alluring you are, how sexy you are?" Of course not! We all need and want that periodic confirmation that indirectly says we are recognized, appreciated and valued. Well, men are no different. That's why a woman who acknowledges his brilliance and his amazing abilities as a reflection of who he is, will grab his attention: married or not.

Centerpiece

Have you heard the term "wallflower"? Well... Don't be one! Instead, be the centerpiece, the beautiful flower that stands in the middle of the room and to which eyes are drawn to. A woman who chooses to be a centerpiece is confident, self-assured and attractive. She doesn't need to be a raving beauty, but she does need to know how to make the most of what she's got. Her confidence and attitude make up for the rest of what she does not physically have, and allows her to change like a chameleon in the eyes of the beholder.

It doesn't matter how big or small she is. I have seen every type of woman achieve this "centerpiece" status. It's somewhat similar to being a hostess at someone else's party. How do you do it? You start by following these steps:

1. Look Good.

What qualifies as good for one person varies for another. What works for one person's physical appearance may not necessarily work for another. Don't push the hard fashion trend, if it doesn't do you justice. If you are concerned about your legs, don't wear short skirts that focus on your legs. If you are self-conscious about wearing low-cut tops because you don't want to draw any additional attention to your breasts; don't. Clothing is all about what makes you feel comfortable. If it makes you feel self-conscious or uncomfortable, then what you're wearing is not doing its job.

2. Complete the Little Things.

Complete your physical appearance by doing all the little extras, like polishing your toes as well as your finger nails. I'm sure you remember the movie "Boomerang" and how Eddie Murphy kept meeting beautiful women, but constantly kept checking their toes? Well, that's not just happening in the movies. It's not enough to be pretty.

Ladies, if you are going to wear short, short anything (a dress, a mini-skirt, etc.), please shave your legs. There is nothing less attractive then a pretty woman with great legs in a short dress with leg hair longer than Godzilla's. Yep, you are probably thinking, you don't do that, but believe me, what you can't see, everybody else can. Don't make the mistake of underestimating the vision of an interested man. Believe me, there eyes don't just pop out of there heads in the cartoons. When they are looking, they are REALLY looking. So, don't forget the important little extras to polish off and complete your look.

2. Don't Bring that Attitude In Here.

If you are going to a place to party, take your party attitude with you. Now, I'm not referring to whether you will or will not sleep with someone that evening. I'm talking about being pleasant. If people wanted to be depressed, they could have stayed home and done it for FREE!

Smile and attempt to have fun. You don't need to pour it on or be phony. I'm just saying "leave your worries on the doorstep", BEFORE you go into the club, and just try to have a good time. You might surprise yourself and actually have fun.

3. Mingle.

Now we are getting into some of the more difficult steps. However, you really will not believe how easy this is. You don't need to know anyone. Although, this entire process is easier if you have at least one of your girlfriends there or one person you can feel comfortable circulating back to, just in case you feel you need to. Again, remember, all of the people at the party would not have come out unless they wanted to meet people and have a good time. So, all you need is a little nudge to get you started, and just a touch of daring. So, I will give you a few tips on how to get started.

a. Pick a Moderately Attractive Guy. Look around and find a guy that you consider to be not too attractive. Now, I know I'm going to hear it now from the men. But, let's get real. Is a moderately attractive guy really going to turn away a good-looking woman? Not likely. And if he does, do you really care? In the back of your mind, you're thinking "Hell, I was doing him a favor!" You see how easy it is to bounce back from the defeat of a moderately attractive guy's rejection. Whereas, if you started with the cream of the crop, and got rejected, you would probably be a bit crushed, especially if it was your first time trying to "mingle".

So, approach Mr. Okay first, and start-up a conversation. You do this to build your confidence. A moderately attractive guy should feel privileged to talk to a pretty woman. Your chances of rejection are almost 100% guaranteed NOT to happen. You will also find, surprisingly enough, that guys, as a whole, are not as harsh in saying "no" as women are. I think it's because they've had to do the asking for so long, that they truly understand what it takes to make that long walk across the floor.

Back to "the mingle": so, talk to your first chosen person until you feel comfortable, or you get the signal that he wants to move on.

b. Move On. Always leave them wanting more of your conversation, and more of your attention. You never want to stay long enough were they feel they don't want to talk to you again. You want to hit it and move onto the next person. That way you leave him with a pleasant memory, but you didn't stay long enough to were out your welcome.

So, when you have completed this first step of mingling, you can move onto the next person. But the advantage you have now created, is that you now know one more person at the party. So, now, if your girlfriend is busy, you can always pass this guy on the way to the bar or on the way to rest your feet and just say, 'hello" or make a quick reference to something he told you about before. It makes you look like you really know people at this party when you don't. You really only know him and your girlfriend. Also, it makes you appear comfortable in this environment, even though you aren't.

c. Intercept a Group of Men. Now you can repeat step one of mingling over and over again or you can move on to the next step of mingling. It really depends on the party, your comfort level and what would best suit your purpose at the party. If you're ready, the next step is to jump into a conversation with a group of men who are not really too heavily involved in conversation. Unless you've had a lot of experience doing this, you shouldn't be trying to interrupt a conversation that is really moving along, only to jump in and slow it down because you know nothing about the topic. It's not that you can't do it. It's just that it requires a little more experience in mingling. So, you look for a small group of men that are just generally talking, and introduce yourself.

If you can, you might confess why you decided to jump into their group when there are other people around. You look for why they stand out and tell them. Don't lie too grandly. Guys like comments that will pump up their egos, but they can also smell, pure bull shit. So, make sure you give them either the truth or a well coated "pill" (a lie coated with a slight truth; we will discuss this in the chapter entitled, The Art of Lying).

Once you have met them, you now know two or three more people. You just keep doing this. Again, if you pass one of them on your way to a new location and he is standing doing nothing, stop and say "hello" again or stop and ask a quick question and then move on.

d. Ask People to Dance. Again, you can start by asking one of the less attractive men to dance, while you are in the wake of the initial conversations. I know men are not too crazy about me saying that a woman should ask a not-so attractive guy to dance first and then work her way up, but let's be honest. Guys do this too. I discovered that men are not as naïve as they would like for you to believe to this practice, when I saw the movie "How to be a Player".

Try to have a good time and even if a guy says, "no" to a dance, it doesn't mean that the conversation must end. But be aware of his body language; that will let you know if you are staying too long or if you need to move on. Remember, you really are not trying to out stay your welcome. You just want to move around the party.

e. Give Respect. If you find a guy that wants to "nest" (camp out at your side) because he's uncomfortable, you don't need to be rude. Just say that you've got to go catch up with your friends for a while but you will save him a dance later, and smile as you leave. Remember, he needs to save face just like you do. Don't embarrass him, just because you're now feeling comfortable and now have the upper hand. Give respect; get respect. You may not want to stay with him all evening, but if you feel he is harmless and will not stick to you like glue, you can return the favor, by just popping through for a quick second and saying, "Hello," so he won't feel so alone.

f. Circulate. It's like the song says, "A party's not a party 'til it's ran all through". So, don't forget to circulate, not once, not twice, but several times. Why? Because you want to see what your new options are on the other sides of the club. People will come and go and your options will change every 10 minutes, if not sooner. You want to see and be seen. The last thing you want is for some attractive guy to come up to you right before you have to leave, and tell you that he saw you once, lost you in the crowd and had been looking for you all night. Unfortunately, you were on the other side of the club in a corner...all night.

g. Make Them Feel Welcome. You think I'm kidding, but I'm not. As you circulate around the club, make your new acquaintances and your old ones feel welcome, even though you just saw them 30 minutes ago. People like to feel special (like Janet Jackson says, "Everyone has the need to feel special") and a smile can do that. If you see an old friend, don't be afraid to show affection by giving a hug, not to mention it makes him look good. Don't be afraid to be happy. Relax a bit.

h. Reach For the Stars. There may be one special guy that you decide you want to meet. After you have built up your confidence, you might be willing to bite the bullet and take a chance by introducing yourself. Remember, he doesn't have anything to gain by being mean to you. To the contrary, people are watching him too. If he can't be at least nice, then it could hurt him more than it could hurt you. And if that's his attitude, you don't want him, nor do you have to wonder any more about what would have been. You know exactly what would have happened, because it did. NOTHING!

On a more positive note, he could be a nice person that is not approached often for the same reason that you almost didn't introduce yourself; people are afraid to approach him because he's attractive and he's hesitant to approach others because he's a bit shy and fears rejection himself. It doesn't matter much. You have to keep in mind, that you are not there to find a husband or a wife, you are there to meet people and have fun. And if you ARE there to find a husband, you have come to the wrong place.

4. You Give, Now It's Time To Receive.
You will not believe how people have been watching. While you've been walking around mingling and dancing with the moderately attractive guys, the more attractive ones were checking you out. The advantage to this is that you may feel a little uncertain about approaching the really hot men (extremely attractive or FINE), but now, some of them will approach you. Why? Because that good-looking guy is just as concerned about being rejected as anyone else. If he sees that you are fun and that you can have fun with anyone, he knows he's got a good chance of not being embarrassed by you acting stupid or pretending that you're on a high horse. You've shown that you are approachable and that's important. I promise you; this works!

Express Yourself

"You know life? It's all about expression. You only live once and you're not coming back; so, express yourself."

-- **Salt 'n' Pepa**

There are women who are afraid of simply be who they are. The concern is that someone may not like who you are. Some of us (both men and women) can be so concerned and hesitant about showing who we truly are that we change factors about ourselves to the point that we end up displaying an image of someone we are not. Or as Chris Rock said, "...when people first meet, people aren't meeting us [who we really are] anymore, they are meeting our representative [the illusion we present of ourselves]." However, think about what it would mean for a person to feel free to be who we are. Now, I am not talking about, unbuckling the belt on your pants, sitting in front of the television with a box of chocolates, while you belch from eating with record speed. I am talking about sharing who you really are with someone. If you did that, you would at least have a 50% chance of another person actually wanting to be with the person you actually are. I say 50%, because they can only say, "yes" or "no".

I've got a question: Who is more attractive, a beautiful woman who sits across the room giving a guy eye contact or an attractive woman who takes the initiative to walk up to a man and tell him how sexy he makes her feel and how great he looks and how masculine he is?

The answer is, the woman who expresses herself. Why? Men get tired of always having to be the first to initiate interest or be the one responsible for making all the moves. As a result, it becomes attractive to be approached by a woman who is making all, if not some, of the effort. In a round about way, it says that he was so strikingly appealing that she felt compelled to take the first step to make sure that he didn't get away. And that is an attractive thought. It would be for a woman who is approached by a man. So, why wouldn't it be for a man who is approached by a woman?

Now don't get me wrong, there are actually some men who feel threatened by women taking initiative. But that is more so targeted toward aggressiveness, not initiative. So, what do guys think about women approaching them? I asked twenty men (from five states) this question and these were the sum of their responses:

First Response: Daniel (25-year old male from IL): "It would be nice, if a woman approached me every once in a while. I get tired of always being the one to make the effort."

Second Response: Sam (31-year old male from NJ) "Women do. I get approached all the time. I don't see it as any big deal."

The third guy seemed to have a lot to say. Third Response: Kevin (28-year old male from CA) "I don't have a problem picking someone up every night I go out. I find it somewhat amusing that women think that only one woman in the club is giving me a sexy look. I can stand in one place for about three minutes and point out at least three women giving me that "come over" here look that is suppose to be so alluring. Who I pick is not a matter of who I like best because, I don't know any of them. Some nights I feel like [I want] a brunette. Some nights I feel like picking up a blonde. I'm like a kid in a candy store. I've got my pick of anyone. Would I mind if some woman came up to me? No. Would it increase her chances of getting my attention? Maybe. When I go to a club, I'm not looking for a wife. I'm looking for someone that can make my night feel complete [with sex]. That's all."

More importantly, than "What if he doesn't like my initiative?" you should ask yourself these other questions:

Who are you?

I ask this question, because, if you are a person that believes in taking initiative, why would you want to change and pretend to be someone you're not? The problem with not being yourself is even if you do attract a guy by being timid, you could loose him in the middle or near the end because you were not who he thought you were. And how could you be happy with someone that would not allow you to openly be who you are? There is something very limiting about being with someone who can't appreciate significant parts of your personality or your total overall being.

Who do you want to be?

I ask this question because, <u>you</u> need to know the answer. Are you the type of person that has been going to clubs and bars all of your life and who waits for everyone else to make the first move only to be approached by guys that are not at the top of your "A-list"? If so, are you content with that? Have you been burning inside to make a move to initiate conversation with some very attractive guys, but just haven't found the nerve?

What are you willing to settle for?

Someone once said that ..."the definition of insanity is to repeatedly perform the same tasks or activities and to keep expecting different results". If your previous method of trying to get a guy isn't working, then you and I both know that you have to change the actions to get different results.

Make the first move. Give it a shot. Think about it this way: it cannot possibly be any worse than it is now. Nothing great was ever gained without a little bit of sacrifice, and in this instance, your sacrifice would be a little bit of your comfort level.

On the other hand, if what you have is good enough and you would be happy to spend the rest of your life with it, then feel content to stay exactly as you are. But if you want more, if you dream of being with a better person who you feel you have possibly missed because of your inability to take a chance, you've got to grab a piece of your destiny by the reigns and tell it you're going to take over the ride from here. In a nutshell: "Ask the guy to dance! He can only say 'yes' or 'no'. You can think of it as a

50% chance he'll say 'no' or you could think of it as a 50% chance he'll say 'yes'!

The Fear of Rejection

You would think that guys are comfortable with rejection from women, but they are not. In fact, rejection for men tends to have a cumulative effect. Being rejected many times (in a very rude manner, especially) can make them hesitate to approach women in the future. Women, on the other hand, sit back and wait to be "hunted" during the course of "The Hunt". However, while women are in the driver's seat, their wait-and-come-find-me mentality leaves them with whatever decides to wait and come find them.

Last year, I spoke with several women. One of which (Jennifer, a 24-year old) was dating a guy she really liked, but eventually had some problems connecting with and eventually separated. She wanted to call him and work out their problems, but was afraid that he would not want to. She was also afraid that if she made the first move and he wasn't interested, that she would look like a fool. After she told us her story, I told them one about a woman I had met about 2 years ago.

Kari was a friend of a friend that I had met at a conference. She approached and told me about how she was in love with this particular man. She was only 22 years of age, and he was 23. They would occasionally meet to do small things together.

She knew there was something special there for her. The feeling she got from talking to him, and spending time with him went beyond any kind of sexual experience she had ever had with a man, but she was afraid to tell him. She was afraid to attempt to move their friendship to a relationship (the Intimacy level) out of fear of rejection. So, she said nothing.

She treasured their friendship so much that she was afraid of challenging it; so, she didn't. She thought, "Well, I will wait and see what happens, let me feel out the situation and see if he is interested in me first". Well, she waited and eventually decided to say and do nothing.

A year went by and she dated other men. However, no man ever gave her the same tingling feeling that her one special guy did. So, she thought about contacting him again. As a result, they occasionally spoke by phone and she slowly tried to let him know that she could be interested in him as more than a friend. She was, of course, testing the waters. After a few months, he called her and said that he would be in town at the end of the month.

She thought, "Okay, I'm going to take this to the next level when he gets into town".

She was still somewhat uncomfortable about moving forward, but knew that she would have to make a stronger move.

Well, the day came when he was to be in town, yet she did not get a phone call. She didn't know what time he was coming in. She didn't know if she should pick him up at the airport, meet him at the airport for a layover, meet him at his hotel, or even if he wanted to crash at her place. But, she thought, he will let her know when he gets into town. But a day passed, then two, then three and no phone call. She began to think, "I guess he wasn't able to stop through. Maybe he got a straight through flight and he will call when he gets home."

Well, about 2 weeks later she received a call from a close girlfriend, and after they shot the breeze with girl talk for a while, her girlfriend finally said, did you hear about Tim?" (Tim was the person she was suppose to have met 2 weeks ago.)

"No, what news," she replied.

"He died last week"

She was shocked and in disbelief, but it was later confirmed. Tim was dead. They said that it was a virus that he caught. It initially was not a concern, but quickly took a turn for the worst.

The irony is that she thought time was guaranteed for the two of them because they were so young. But she found out the hard way that time is guaranteed to no one, not even the young. The sad truth is that she had allowed her fear of rejection, of a momentary awkward feeling, to now impact her life. And what she thought was an awkward moment had instead become an uncertainty for a lifetime.

Why? Because, now she will always wonder about what could have been, what should have been and what wasn't. Also, she compares that feeling that he gave her in the absence of sex, to every man that she meets. The price of not acting was high. But everyone has to make his or her own decisions.

When faced with the potential to have more, but you don't because you hesitate, you have got to ask yourself these questions:

1. Is the potential of what I believe I could have, greater than the momentary embarrassment I could suffer, from an awkward situation of asking this question?

2. If he says that he is not interested, do I have a method in mind to bounce back?

3. Lastly, I like to ask the last question: If this could have been something special, am I prepared to spend the rest of my life wondering about what I could have had?

I know what my answer would be every time, but it is all a matter of what you are willing to settle for and what you fear.

Chapter 3

The Players

■ ■ ■

I Got GAME!

Just as a basketball player can have the right moves to manipulate and call the shots in the game, so can a player within the Mating Game.

"Oh, I GOT GAME!" doesn't just apply to sports anymore and can be frequently heard out in the Mating arena. To proclaim that you've GOT GAME when it comes to the Mating Game means that you've acquired a few moves of your own to call the shoots, and those shots aren't just necessary when you're single.

During one group discussion, a woman in her mid-30's named Karen told me that her husband's secretary had been trying to move in closer with her husband. His secretary had done things like borrow money from him and used it as an excuse to talk on a personal level, but always brought in large bills that he couldn't break so that the saga of the "lunch money" could continue. As a result, her husband and his secretary had had several friendly discussions. The wife went out to visit her husband at work on one particular day and the secretary asked if she could meet his wife. Not thinking much about it, he said yes and brought the secretary out to the car to meet his wife. Well, after that, the wife knew that the secretary was making moves to move in closer and she decided that that wasn't going to happen.

I'm sure that her husband thought that the entire situation was purely friendly, until one evening when the husband came home from work. He was confronted with a rude awakening. The wife told her husband that his secretary had called her at home (earlier that day) and told her that she was interested in her husband and that there was nothing that she could do about it. He, of course, couldn't believe that the secretary would do that, especially when it had been nothing more than a friendly relationship, to him.

"Why would your secretary call me and say that, if there's nothing going on?" his wife said.

Her husband was surprised that his secretary would cause problems. So, the husband stopped the friendly conversations with his secretary and the two of them went back to the formal work relationship they had had before.

Why am I telling you this story? If you guessed that the secretary NEVER called! You were right. The secretary never called the house. However, the wife didn't need an actual incident to see where this was heading and what the secretary was trying to do. She also didn't need an actual call to create the effect that his secretary had called. Yes, girlfriend, GOT GAME!

Now, we all know that the best way to play any game, is to know who the other players are. That helps us to better understand what their goals are in playing, and that can be very important. Knowing this type of information can put you at an advantage in the Mating Game. So, we have to ask...

Who is He?

"Life's a drag... or maybe, <u>he's</u> just a drag..."

You've heard of a Drag Queen? I'm sure you have. Well, have you ever thought of people as being in drag? I know I have. No, I don't mean that people, in general, just walk around in brightly colored clothing and high heels! I mean the way people are now, the way people dress every day, that's their drag. What am I talking about? Well, when you first think of the term "drag", you immediately think about its reference to a person's costume or dress, right? Well, I once heard someone say that everyone is in drag all the time. By this they meant that everyone is putting on a show and pretending to be someone that they either are, want to be or wish they were. I've heard some people jokingly refer to a business suit as a monkey suit, making a correlation between the monkey that use to sit on top of the musician's music box and dance for money, giving a show, performing. It's the same thing.

So, with that mental picture in mind, it would naturally follow that when you go to work, you're in drag to play the role of a more concerned professional person. Do you see it now? When you go out to a club, you're in drag to present a more party-flavored image. When you go to church, you are, again, still in drag to present a more conservative and spiritual image and when you go to a formal gathering, you are in drag to present someone of culture, substance or importance.

Is it all about the clothes? No. It is also the attitude behind the clothes. The clothing just sets the mood or the tone and is a part of our daily wardrobe that we need to play our everyday roles in society and in life.

So, if everybody is in drag, it means that everyone is pretending, right? Almost. It means that everyone is pretending or displaying the part of themselves that they want us to see at that moment. And with that in mind, let's look at some of the people we meet in drag when we attempt to socialize.

Player Pete.
Every guy wants to be a player. And Player Pete is the one they claim to be, the player of choice. So, what do they do? They dress up to play the role. They get into drag to play a character, much like that of a performer in a theatrical production. He puts on the suit and the shoes that show him as stylish or slightly flashy. He gets his hair cut to match and, of course, we can't stop there. He knows he has got to have the clean, shiny new car (a prop) to whisk you away in. Why? Oh, please, we know why! Because women love nice cars. Then comes the attitude. The "I-am-exciting, fun, confident, ready and have a wallet-full-of-money-to-sweep-you-away" attitude.

This is of course the mistake that we make. We put too high an emphasis on the drag. So much so, that we forget about our Standards under the Qualifiers (the minimum requirements for boyfriend status) and can't see Player Pete for what he is, a player, nothing more, but quite possibly something less. He is not that special and not that great. He can promise you a moment of feeling special, but tomorrow, "Don't call me, I'll call you."

Pete is sexually adventurous and we like that; don't we ladies. Pete can show you some new tricks, along with the old favorites. He is ready to have a good time and if you want to be the one, it could be you tonight that he will feed his lines. But don't expect a future with Pete. You will not get the house, the car, the children and a life with this one. He is a creature of the night looking for prey, and unfortunately everyone wants to be next.

What's Wrong With That?

Women who interact with Pete love the excitement and the spontaneity that Pete provides. Most women who have fun with Pete will tell you that they are just out to have fun, constantly confessing "It's okay, if it's just for one night". The truth is, that that's not exactly true. Yep, the first couple of times the sex is great, but after a while, you begin to want more and that's when you get hurt by Player Pete. He views sex as a commodity for the taking, and if you're willing to provide it, ...what can I say?

Pete is caught up in the Hunt stage of the Mating Game and if you're willing, he will provide you with the greatest sex you've ever had. But if you're expecting the sex to turn into love with a Player Pete, you're wasting your time. That will only happen when and if Pete decides to move onto the next level of a relationship. But, never-the-less, women keep trying to convert Pete to a one-woman man, and Pete just keeps lovin' the life he's livin' and all the women that keep trying to change him.

Busy Dick.
You might know him better as, "My Baby's Daddy" or "My Baby's Fatha". Busy Dick got his name honest. He is just what I said, busy. He use to be care-free Player Pete, but Pete don't take to responsibility too well, you know, like protected sex. I once had a Player Pete tell me that he didn't use condoms because he could just look at a woman and tell if she was infected by HIV.

Allow me now to take a moment and sway from the subject to address this statement. Let me tell you what I told him. I told him he was losing it, because while everyone said that HIV didn't discriminate, it did. You think I'm lying. HIV is a pretty people's disease! Therefore, HIV discriminates against the ugly. Oh, you might be laughing, but HIV is sexually transmitted, so that means the more times you have sex, the greater the opportunity for HIV to be contracted. So, WHO do you think has a greater chance of having HIV? A pretty person or an ugly person? I rest my case.

If his attitude about sex didn't prove that he was unconcerned and uncaring, then his attitude about having children did. I met a Busy Dick once who actually told me, "I want you to have my baby." I guess I was suppose to ignore the other two babies he already had by two other mothers. Ladies, I just couldn't do it. I told him that I just wasn't "Baby Motha Material."

Two years later someone gave me an update on him. I heard that now he's got to keep 2 jobs and one on the side to care for the 3 babies he's got from 3 different women. Yep, I said 3. He couldn't get me to take off the condom, so he went to someone who would and now that moment of pleasure is lasting him (and her) another 18 years. You would think that his three 18 year old commitments would slow him down; wouldn't you? But it doesn't. Well, if it did, he wouldn't be a Busy Dick anymore, would he?

What's Wrong With That?

The mistake that women make with Busy Dick is that they think a baby will trap him. But people like Busy Dick are unfazed by a child. Few men are now days, because (of course) we all know that you shouldn't get married just because you are having a child anymore. Those days of becoming an outcast because you're having a child out of wedlock are over. Hell, they've got sperm banks now for the woman who intentionally wants to get pregnant and become a single mother.

However, more importantly, there are still women that think a child is going to bring out the best in a man, show him how important a family is and love her all the way to the alter. But those endings only happen in the movies and even the directors have to yell, "Cut!" at some point. Then, the music along with the fantasy is over. If there is a lesson to be learned about Busy Dick, it is that you cannot trap him (or any other man, for that matter) with responsibility, when it was a lack of responsibility that he's obviously guilty of now. And despite all that we know about AIDS, HIV Child Support and STD's, many Busy Dicks still don't wear condoms. NBA stars and Rock singers are dropping babies left and right in state after state continuing to populate the world. These people are Busy Dicks and definitely true to their names.

Love 'um & Leave 'um Lennie.
Lennie is out shopping. He is just maxing and relaxing. He's not thinking about the complications of a real relationship. You know this because, when a complication occurs, that's when he's leaving.

At first sight, one would think that Lennie is a nice guy. He is sweet, caring, charming but he is not prepared for commitment or challenge.

I had a friend who met a Lennie. He was her dream come true. She had had a hard time meeting guys that were really about something and when she met Lennie, she thought this was it. Life was great for her, at first. She use to call him on the phone every night; you know...that lovie dovie stuff. They use to go to places of common interest, like the museum and happy hours.

Well, pretty soon, my friend wanted to take the relationship a little further. All of a sudden, Lennie is saying that she is calling too much, that she spends too much time with him. Nothing had changed really. But now the same events that once brought them both pleasure had taken on a different meaning. They had switched from mere fun and companion*ship* to slight commitment and relation*ship*. And that was not a "*ship*" that Lennie wanted to sail.

So, Lennie started causing friction. It was a means to an exit. A method of escape. "You are too this..." and "You are too that ..." he would tell her and then I would have to listen to that (through her) in the wee hours of the night.

"Thank you, Lennie!!" I'm being sarcastic, of course.... Why would I say that? Because then she started thinking that she was a completely flawed person and yes, I had to listen to that too. It took her a while to get back to normal, but women always do. That's why people don't look at Lennie as being so bad. But the price of wallowing in self-doubt and confusion for the six months, that she paid, was a little stiff, considering she had only had 3 months of happiness. That's what happens when you "fall" into so-called love with Lennie. With both eyes

WIDE shut (hint-hint: that movie), you stumble into a complication that is mistakenly defined as a relationship, with Love 'um and Leave 'um Lennie.

What's Wrong With That?

Lennie is not in it for the long haul. He is here today and gone tomorrow. A relationship with Lennie seems perfect initially until reality hits and then Lennie is not to be seen. Lennie is not living in reality, he is living in a fantasy world of perfection. Relationships initially seem like a fantasy with Lennie because they are fun and new and there is so much that you don't know about each other. But, after the newness wears off, Lennie is gone.

You are probably thinking, "Now, Anita! How could she have known that she was with a Lennie?" The answer is, his history. Lennie always has a history of leaving women abruptly and under the worst of terms. However, when a Lennie tells a woman how his last girlfriend was CRAZY or OBSESSIVE, she wants to believe that the fault lies totally with his ex-girlfriend and that Lennie was completely innocent of any wrong doing...but we know it takes two!

Somehow, despite the negative stuff Lennie tells us about his past women, we want to believe that all Lennie needs is a GOOD woman, and a little TLC (tender loving care), which some woman is always willing to provide. There are always women there to provide Lennie with a constant pool of applicants, to hurt and eventually leave. So, listen to his history as it unfolds, and see the future that he holds for you, if you decide to be with a Lennie.

Wham, Bam thank-you Sam.

Sam is only interested in meeting you for sex. There is no relationship, there is no cuddling, there is no let's do something together. There is only a pathway full of one-nighters.

Now some women appreciate that, especially since they know that a Sam is not really about anything that they would really want to get with. Most women consider Sam to be a necessary evil. You know what I'm talking about. Some people need to have sex at least once a week, others claim to once a month, some can go longer, but when you reach the breaking point, Sam knows you're going to come looking for him. And as he puts it, "I'll [He'll] be there to provide a much needed service."

Sam is, as Steve Harvey put it in his HBO Comedy Special, your Mandingo Man. Sam is there to drop by for your regular visit and then... "get the Hell out," as another woman finished. Tonda, a 37-year old woman from Chicago continued, "Relationships take time, and that's the one thing I don't really have right now. I am very busy and don't want to be bothered with the complications of what he did or what I said [issues that are generally found in an on-going relationship]. The easy answer is to get a Sam and change him like a leased car when it has exceeded the acceptable level of mileage."

Sam may or may not have a job. He moves from woman to woman with such frequency to complete his rounds that he has little time for anything else. Chances are he has become the flavor of the month for one of many and will be staying with her for a few weeks to be at her beck and call. The other women are not forgotten, they just get the time that is left over. After a while, his time with his Lady Of The Month will expire, but no need for alarm, he has already picked out his next lady (in waiting) to carry him for the following month. She is usually all lined up and ready to go. It doesn't take much, just a little more attention. They both know it is not a permanent arrangement, unless some other complication comes into play. But Sam will never be true to one woman. He is a frequent shopper of women and would not even consider giving up his many LAYdies.

What' Wrong With That?

Nothing, if you are just in it for sex...but no woman really ever is. Sam is excellent in bed; but he should be, he has had enough experience to impress anyone, if he were to ever document it in detail on a resume. Again, the problem with getting involved with a Sam is that you may not be in touch with your reality. Sam, is NOT your knight in shining armor. He is not ready to be married nor is he marriage material. Some women get caught up in the sex, and start to feel that they are running out on time and believe that Sam fulfills all of their needs, when he really only fulfills ONE.

If you just want sex, go forth and be merry with Sam. But, if you are kidding yourself, you can really get hurt playing around with a Sam.

Sporty Scott.

Scott is a true sports fan. He not only has one sport that he particularly loves, but he is a sportsman himself. Usually, he grew up with a sport as a child and that passion and respect for the joy that the sport brought to his life has made him addicted to physical activity, of all kinds.

Sports transformed his body into something that women wanted, made him respected by the guys and made women take notice. Now, he's just following through in allowing himself to be adored. What woman doesn't love a well tuned body, with muscles (pronounced "muss-cals"). To see the true curves in a male form that is treated as a temple is to behold a work of art. He is an Adonis, straight off the pages of Greek mythology, only in color. The only problem is that he knows what he is and knows what people want and he uses women to get his quick fix. What's that? Sex, pleasure, variety and anything else he might demand.

Scott will also use his dedication to his sport as an excuse for not spending as much time with you. But in reality, he is spending it finding other women.

What's Wrong With That?

Scott is just having fun. He is like a child, with his hand in the candy jar. The only problem is that the jar is bottomless and allows him to have an endless supply of sweets (you...along with every other woman in the world). He is not interested in looking beyond next month. Scott is just out to have a good time. Unfortunately, it's at your expense.

Fun Phil.

A while ago, I co-wrote a column for a magazine. A person wrote me asking why women say they want a GOOD man (who has a job and is dedicated to a single woman), but don't go after such a man. In short, the writer of the question, felt he was all of these things that women claim to want. Yet, he had no women falling all over themselves to go out with him. The answer is that women crave and want excitement and FUN, and sometimes stability alone is just plain boring! People need excitement. Women need fun, and a Fun Phil is just the one willing to provide it.

Phil will pop in, show a woman a good time, take her places she has never been and then disappear. He is adventurous! He is spontaneous and he is fun. Fun Phil will take you to a 4 star restaurant that you didn't know existed. Phil will take you kite flying on a beautiful Sunday morning at the top of the highest point in the city or to a Saturday night party at a health club at midnight. However, Fun Phil is not into commitment at all. He lives in the moment to enjoy life, and women love to vibe off his excitement and energy. However, if a woman ever tried to take a care-free spirit like a Fun Phil down the path of a serious relationship, Phil would be out of there faster than you could say "fun".

What's Wrong With That?

Phil is a playboy and a party guy, not much unlike Scott, but instead of sports being Phil's passion, fun and excitement are. Phil is again a temporary fix, he is not thinking long-term, he is only thinking about tomorrow and next week. That can be a very exciting time, if you are the object of such spontaneity, but he is not a long-term guy.

I know, I know, everyone wants to tame a Scott or a Phil because what woman doesn't want to share their excitement and zest for life on a daily basis. A Phil helps to make each day a little more pleasant, a little more exciting. So, what's wrong with him? He's not real. Everybody has shortcomings and problems; that's the reality of it. Phil is fine for tonight and tomorrow, but Phil is not the person that will help you save for your IRA or who will mutually invest in property to plan for the future. Phil is here, now and today...only.

Dollar Bill.

Bill is the guy who went to graduate school and is now a doctor, a lawyer or something that produces some means of finance for his many romances. Women see an attractive, sharp, dressed man (as ZZ Top put it) and they immediately think "money"! And Dollar Bill is the one who has got it and is fully willing to spend it, but do not be mistaken. Dollar Bill is buying something. He is buying your hottest sex, your passion, and sometimes your mind and if you let him, a piece of your heart. Bill can be dangerous to those that allow themselves to fall victim to the Dollar Bill. Fact is, we could control our obsession with the Dollar Bill, but who wants to? So, instead we relinquish that power, that control, to the whim of a Bill.

That is a BIG Mistake! But that's a lesson learned from experience. However, on the other hand playing with Dollar Bill could get you money in the end to finance a dream. A certain PYT (i.e.: as Michael Jackson put it back in the day for "Pretty Young Thing") who had a two-year fling with a Dollar Bill who was a star of a top television situation comedy, is now featuring her new clothing line in a series of big time department stores, to include Macy's. Some women play to get paid, and do...with a Dollar Bill.

What's Wrong With That?
Bill makes money and money makes the world go round. For women, money is power. If you give her some money, she will give you her power, and that is what Dollar Bill is counting on every time. However, money only has power if it can buy what you want with it, and too many woman are ready to sell. So, until the market closes, Dollar Bills will always be in high demand.

Unlike Phil and Scott, Bill is planning for the future; it's just that that future doesn't include you. Bill is almost everything you want a man to be, but a Dollar Bill is not faithful. Cheating is an expensive hobby and Bill's got the cash to bank roll the venture. However, despite it all, many women will acknowledge that and attempt to catch a Dollar Bill despite how demeaning it may be. Bill isn't interested because he's having too much fun. He has worked hard and is probably a part of the "work hard, play hard" group. Also, Bill is an uncertain bet to place your money on; however, no matter. Most women will bet on him anyway. Still, it never ceases to amaze me what a woman will do for a Dollar Bill.

Gay Guy.
Guy is exactly as he appears, ...*Gay*. So, why is any woman after him? Come on NOW! He dresses well, he loves to shop, he loves to talk and he's usually extremely attractive. There's just one little, tiny problem....he isn't interested in having sex... with a WOMAN, any woman! Hmmm. ...and that's not good. Ironically, enough, women love Gay Guy for the very reason that we can never be with him, because he's not interested in us for sex.

If Gay Guy likes you, and spends time with you and allows you to be a part of his world, a woman KNOWS that it's not because he wants to do some horizontal dirty dancing. In fact, I'm sure that that's the furthermost thing from his mind. Yes. If Gay Guy likes you, you know it's because he genuinely likes YOU. You have to admit that's kind of appealing and somewhat attractive.

He is everything a woman wants in a relationship, ...with the exception of sex. Some women have had such a hard time finding a wonderful heterosexual guy, that they are willing to create one. Face it Gay Guy has all of the makings of a wonderful guy. He's sensitive, listens and isn't afraid to display his emotions. He's so perfect that some women are willing to give up the element of sex in order to get everything else!

However, they are also certain that they can change Gay Guy to Heterosexual Guy. And that's really outrageous, but more than that, it's silly. Obviously, his sexual orientation is his decision and his alone. You can't make a gay guy, heterosexual any more than you can make a heterosexual guy, gay. Since a woman doesn't have the right equipment (sexually...) to be in a full-fledged relationship with Gay Guy, he is bound to either stray or leave. And even if the world stopped and Gay Guy changed his sexual preference, just for her, would he ultimately be happy? Probably not. Her desire to change him is a selfish one and a bit ironic. I mean, look at it.

She wants him because he appreciates and respects her for who she is and yet she doesn't respect him enough to appreciate him for who he is, a Gay Guy! If her respect for him was genuine, she would want what's best for him and that would be to let him be who he is...gay.

What's Wrong With That?

The conversion, better known as the act of trying to convert gay guy to heterosexual guy, is an act of desperation that many of us still attempt. And although we didn't quite see that happening with Julia Roberts in the movie, "My Best Friend's Wedding", we could definitely see the female attraction to Gay Guy.

It is easy to fall into a relationship with Gay Guy. He doesn't want anything from you, other than your friendship; it makes you think "Damn, why can't more guys be GAY!" But then you realize the reality of what you are saying and that just wouldn't work out for women. Gay Guy is a great friend, but that's what he is: a friend, not a lover, nor a fighter. It's easy to see all of his many qualities, but as a long range project, he is outside of the grasp of reality for women. Eventually, sex, will come into play and that's when the illusion will come crashing down.

Reliable Roy.

Roy works everyday. You know exactly what time he will be home and you know exactly where he is during the course of the day. Initially, women think this is a wonderful thing, but others become bored with how routine it all becomes. There is no excitement, no spontaneity, no change or improvement to look forward to. Women like excitement and improvement every now and then.

Some enjoy it more frequently than others, but every woman wants it.

What's Wrong With That?

Excitement is part of living life. Reliable Roy is a great guy to have; he just needs a bit of coaxing to get him to be a little more adventurous and fun. Player Petes don't corner the market on excitement. A Roy is a wonderful long-term guy to be with. The biggest problem for most relationships is usually money and Roy is out trying to earn it to bring home the bacon for his family. It's not that Roy is not a fun guy, he may just be a little preoccupied with the realities and the day-to-day routine of life. It takes a lot to make a long-term commitment to a woman or a family, and the day-to-day responsibilities can make a man emotionally numb to a woman's need for the extras. While he's just trying to be a good provider and take his life one day at a time, problems can be developing all around him: she becomes bored, she becomes unsatisfied. But Roy could become exciting and fun with a little bit of nudging.

A Reliable Roy I like to recall is Arnold Swatsenhager's character in the movie, "True Lies". Remember how his wife, just wanted to have some excitement in her life? So she started having a non-sexual affair with the car salesman who said he was a secret agent. The irony was that her husband, Arnold, in reality was an exciting secret agent, that was pretending to be a salesman. I think every Roy has the ability to become your own private and exciting secret agent. It's all in providing the right opportunity.

Dominating Dan.

This is the man women enjoy seeing jealous. She thinks it means that he loves her s-o-o-o-o much! ...but instead, it means that he is a monster waiting to happen. Dan is the man that abused women will marry thinking that he is going to be so wonderful and caring. His dominating behavior typically starts in the beginning, then later grows into something ugly. It usually is somewhat of a complement to be fussed over. To have someone want you so much that he wants to know where you are at every moment of the day. But these illusions can change quickly to become abusive: emotionally and physically.

What's Wrong With That?

Dan is dangerous. He again creates this illusion of concern that initially appears wonderful. It's great to feel wanted and desired, but Dan can become dangerously possessive or be a pedophile in disguise, waiting for the right moment to sexually attack your children (boy or girl). Either possibility is unthinkable. The good news, however, is that women can avoid selecting a Dan. The signs are always the same. He is possessive, controlling and dominating. He starts out just a little possessive and bit by bit she learns to accept it. Then the level of his domination grows. When he reaches his full capacity, life can become a living Hell. Leaving a

Dan before, during and after is more than golden; it's necessary.

Romeo Ronnie.
I've met Ronnie many times, but nothing can compare to the time I met Ronnie on a talk show.

I'd seen Romeo Ronnie before. Each time he looks completely different. Sometimes he's had black hair and was an African-American. Other times he's had red hair and was English. This time Ronnie had blonde hair. Forever changing, Ronnie aims to please. This time Ronnie was of Norwegian decent, so he had those strong Scandinavian features. And of course, no Romeo Ronnie would be complete without his Juliet, who was there too. And she was just as I had imagined her to be. She was Scandinavian also (this time) with blonde hair: an image straight from the cover of ELLE magazine.

It was incredible to watch how Ronnie worked his Juliet. They were both attractive people, but Ronnie was cunning and manipulative. While Juliet was so trusting and believing, she clung to his every word, much like a puppy walks behind it's master. She was an indentured servant, catering to his every whim and you could tell that he had his cake and was eating it too.

On the air, during the taping of the show, Ronnie never claimed to have any relationship with his Juliet at his side. On the air, he never told Juliet that he loved her or that he cared about her. However, as soon as we went to commercial, he leaned over to Juliet and told her that he did care, she was important to him and that he wouldn't do anything to mess up their relationship. And then he threw in a little bit of confirming reinforcement "And you know this, right?"

When we came back from commercial, I told everybody what Ronnie had done while we were off the air and asked him how many women he had at home that he was also romancing right now. Ronnie looked at me and without saying a word, he gave me the most conceited smile, which said to me, "Many! Yep, your right. You caught me. I'm so proud of myself, because they are all beautiful and they all cling to my every word." He said all of this without making a single sound. So I looked over at Juliet, and found that it was true, she was sitting on the edge of her seat waiting for him to respond, but she was not upset by what I had brought to the attention of the world. She was completely non judgmental, uncommitted to make a break and waiting for her Master to speak.

He looked at me again with an arrogance that I only hoped others could see because it was so subtle, so slight. He knew what he was doing. The entire experience had been a big, humorous joke to Ronnie. And while I saw arrogance, everyone else saw confidence.

After the show was over, it was time to leave. And as all the guests passed to say their good-byes before they left the set, his eyes confronted mine, and with a smirk, his eyes said, "You've lost this round," but everyone else saw charm and charisma.

It was an extremely irritating experience, because Juliet wasn't ready to look at the reality. Even when she looked at me, I could tell she was wearing blinders. She was absent of emotion, completely divorced from the will to make a decision on her own. Ronnie did not pick this Juliet by mistake. He knew exactly what he was doing when he had picked her. And she made a fine addition to his harem. I could feel that thought as they left. I looked at Ronnie one last time to let him know, that the game was not over yet. But that day, he left victoriously.

What's Wrong With That?
Just as Dominant Dan can become physically and mentally abusive, Ronnie is a master at mental manipulation. He will make you feel loved, when he doesn't and he will make you feel special, when you are one of many. No woman, wants to believe she is dating a Ronnie. He seems so caring, so gentle, so romantic and vulnerable. But remember, ladies, a poodle is still a dog too.

Juvenile Joe.
Joe is the guy who walks around telling everybody he's a man. Joe doesn't have a lot of

confidence in who he is. In fact, that's why he's constantly asking everybody who he is, because, he's not sure himself: "Who's the MAN? No, who's the MAN?"

Joe wants to be taken care of. He is basically another child to be included in the head count. Some women like Joe because they feel they can dominate him.

<u>What's Wrong With That?</u>
A man is suppose to be your equal, your partner and that is not what Joe is. Joe is not about responsibility, he is just giving a show, and you can see it if you buy a ticket to the screening of his new movie entitled, "I want to be a Player". But, if you buy a ticket to ride with Joe, there are no refunds or exchanges and most times women just end up plain frustrated. If you have a son by a Joe, you can expect to see a part-time, sometime father. It's not what you want, even if you think it is.

Who am I?

It's only fair to ask the same question of women that I have asked of men. It's really amazing, the changes and the improvements that can be made once you understand who you are in the Mating Game.

In a room full of strangers, it's difficult to admit to a variety of personal short-comings or faults. Besides, it's really nobody's business but your own. However, within the privacy of a book, you are free to read and acknowledge who you are without judgment. And truly, the only one that really needs to know is you, anyway. I, of course, never said I was a Saint and can through, the course of my life, claim many if not all of these roles, including Penny's.

Player Penny.
Penny is of course the female version of Player Pete. She dates many men at the same time; it's amazing how she can keep up with them all. Penny has become a player for one of several reasons. She has either:

- Looked around and decided that a permanent relationship is not possible, so she might as well have fun;
- Decided that she is not going to wait by a phone for some guy to call her, so she is going out to have a good time or,
- Decided: "Hell, I can't find one guy who meets all my Qualifiers; so I'll just create a Variety Sandwich."

Not every Penny is a slut. Penny could just be having fun, with the understanding that she is living in the moment. Some guys, however, tend to get possessive of Penny, ironically enough, because she doesn't want to be possessed. However, ladies, please do NOT read into that statement that if you date lots of guys and are unconcerned about sleeping around that they will want you; it doesn't work that way. If you believe it does, that will be a sure fire recipe for getting used.

  I remember when my name was Penny. I was dating a wide variety of guys. I had nine guys that I dated on a regular basis. I had one guy for when I wanted to be sporty, one guy for when I wanted to have deep conversations, one guy that offered romance, one guy for excitement (he was the bad boy), and one guy for sensitivity (to listen to me), among others. You get the point. I couldn't get all that I wanted in one guy, so I got it out of several. Ironically, it worked just like Steve Harvey said, when he jokingly explained how women can piece together one good man out of several.

  I also remember a couple of the times I got caught. Some might say, a "true player" doesn't get caught, but I beg to differ on that. If you are doing anything long enough, at some point or another, you will get caught. Now, whether people believe what they see is another matter.

  When it comes to the rude awakening of discovering that you were unwillingly played, guys are more calm and rational about the matter. Now, I didn't say they like dating Player Penny or will stand for it; I just said that they are more rational about the situation. Unlike women, when men are unwillingly played, they are more likely to simply leave.

What's Wrong With That?

I have not yet met a Penny who actually became a Player Penny solely for the sex. The truth is it is easier to expect the least from a man and move on. Expecting nothing is a method that prepares her for emotional detachment at all times. It also lessens the impact of the blows or hurt. Because she is always the first one to let go or do the hurting. To expect more would require that she open herself up with the possibility of getting hurt. But, for whatever reason, Penny has decided that she is not going that route and will instead, reject men first, before they can reject her or use him, before he uses her.

The irony is that Player Penny is always getting used, even when she is unaware of it. Because she always wants more, regardless of what she will tell you. But still, she settles for less.

Rebound Babe.

Just as there are women, who always have to have someone in their lives, there are men who require the same. For every man who must have someone, there is a woman willing to take him back and forth whenever he needs her too. Men, like women, will fall back to the woman who will carry and cater to his whims, …while he is looking for someone else. It's not necessarily the "Best of the Last Syndrome". It's more so to fulfill his requirement of not being without a warm body.

Conversely, every Rebound Babe thinks she's in the relationship for the long haul, but she's really just a temporary fix to get him by, until he can find his next woman. Rebound Babe can satisfy his basic needs and has been around long enough to be trained into knowing just how he likes to be satisfied. This is the "Rebound Babe".

He will call her after an unsuccessful night out looking for a new woman for the evening: "I need to come talk to you.", "Can I come over?", "I need to see you." It's just one big "I-I-I-I" "need-need-need" after another. It's all about his needs and his wants. It's really never about you. This is a give and take relationship: she gives and he takes!

The Rebound Babe is the woman that receives the "booty call" (call for sex) late at night. She is the woman that accepts him back under practically any circumstances. Unfortunately, what she might call, unconditional love, he defines as weakness and stupidity. He has tested her, and she has not passed. Therefore, she has now set the tone to be spoken to, used, and treated in any way he chooses.

When I was a Rebound Babe, I always thought I was accepting him back on my terms, and no doubt all the rest believe that too. The reason why being a Rebound Babe will not ever get you into a relationship moving forward is because you have been tested and each time, you have allowed your standards of him (in terms of what is acceptable and what is not) to be lowered. The line goes down further and further with each betrayal only to end up on the floor to be stepped on. As a result, he can do anything, go anywhere with anyone, doing whatever with whomever and still come back to you.

What's Wrong With That?
Rebound Babe, like Player Penny and most of the other women, are controlled predominately by fear. A fear of losing something: respect, face, love or companionship. Fear is the monster that will keep her content with sexually based relationships. Fear is the monster that will make her settle for what he will allow her to have, instead of what she deserves. Fear is dangerous and needs to be confronted, if for no other reason than to tame it and to place it aside so that you may have the life that you deserve, instead of the life that someone is willing to give you.

Not-Now Nancy.
In contrast to Rebound Babe, Not-Now Nancy is more controlling. And it never ceases to amaze me how many Nancys can believe that they can use sex as a method of controlling their husbands. Unfortunately, the problem can be more than just not wanting sex now. It can include the prospect that she truly doesn't enjoy sex. Some Nancys consider it more of a duty and a responsibility than a pleasure. So, she is constantly putting off the issue of making their sex life better. She doesn't want to try new things, because she's content the way things are.

For her, life is routine and anything other than dealing with her relationship with her husband or boyfriend takes priority, even when there are no items requiring immediate attention in her life. She doesn't just put off sex; she puts off many elements of their developing closeness. She becomes predictable, and unconcerned with things at home. In some respects, she acts like a robot. Everything else is more important. This is the woman who believes that marriage marks the victory of the game and no additional effort is required. She puts little to no effort into revitalizing the romance or closeness in her relationship. Her relationship with her husband/boyfriend is secondary and everything else comes first: her girlfriend's problems, her dog's medical appointment. It's procrastination really, and it's that type of procrastination that will send her straight to divorce court or a rude awakening.

This is the woman whose man will be tempted by a "PYT" (Pretty Young Thing) at work. He is starving for attention and affection and there is always someone willing to give it. Unknowingly, Not-Now Nancy has opened a door wide open for someone else to come into the picture and take away her husband, her boyfriend, and alter her family (either temporarily or permanently). And when it happens, she immediately points to how she was taking care of the family and was dedicated to their commitment, when the truth is she was avoiding him all the while and truly helped for this terrible event to occur.

What's Wrong With That?

Nancy is her own worst enemy. She alone creates the problems that she is eventually faced with and she alone can fix the mess she has created. So, how does she fix it?

What seems to be such a simple answer is somewhat of a challenge for a Nancy. If you are a Nancy, take a conscious look at the value of the items you consider to be important in your life and determine if the value and the order really make sense for the long haul. For Nancy, changes need to be made to her priorities and she needs to look at how her actions are impacting her priorities. However, it is also possible that her actions are in fact a self-fulfilling prophecy. She may not have valued the relationship, but couldn't bring herself to end it; so, instead went this route knowing that he would eventually no longer take the abuse and neglect. Thereby, allowing her to take the position of the person done wrong.

Dr. Cindy.

Dr. Cindy is going to make it all better. She's so into taking care of people and trying to help people into becoming something that she wants them to be, that you would think she picked up injured animals along the highway and nursed them back to health when she was younger.

Cindy believes that people can change. She also believes that she can help them change to become a better person. But worst of all she believes that everyone's changing is dependent upon her actions.

Think about it. If someone else took responsibility for things that were not right in your life, would you really need to take control and change? No, you wouldn't. If someone else constantly assumed the responsibility for helping to change you, is the person that's suppose to be changing accepting any of the responsibility for that change? Usually, not.

Dr. Cindy is most often hurting herself along with the person she is suppose to be helping and she is not even aware that she's doing it. The best thing that she could do, is give a man a reason for changing and eventually an ultimatum. And if needed, be prepared to carry out the penalty for not complying with her ultimatum, by leaving. If he chooses not to make that move, then who you have and who you thought you had a relationship with are two different people. Accept it, and move on.

What's Wrong With That?
Unfortunately, what Dr. Cindy doesn't realize is that change is a very personal thing. You cannot make someone change because YOU want or need THEM to change. In fact, the only thing you can do is give someone a reason or a motivation to change for the better and provide them with support in their metamorphosis, but you cannot start it. You cannot push it along and you cannot help to complete it.

People change, because something in their life has happened that has prompted them to change. It is not because of Dr. Cindy. Dr. Cindy actually can prevent a person from changing.

Dr. Cindy never cured anybody. If anyone ever made a change, they did it for themselves and not because of Dr. Cindy. Dr. Cindy believes you can take a piss poor excuse for a man and mold him into the Knight in shining armor she always wanted. Problem is, she is consumed by the devilish role of pushing people to change, which is the very activity that will cause men to push away from Dr. Cindy. "What you see is what you get," is one concept that a Dr. Cindy has not yet absorbed.

People can polish up what was already there, but Cindy is trying to create interest where none existed, complexity where simplicity reigns and long-term goals where here-and-now is the objective. In essence, Cindy tries to take an alligator and make it into a butterfly, but the alligator doesn't have it in him to be a butterfly, nor does he have the desire to be a butterfly. It's not who he is. And that's what's wrong with Dr. Cindy.

Lonely Linda.
Linda is afraid of being by herself. She will do anything not to be alone. She will be in a messed-up relationship, she will stay in an abusive relationship, because just like Dr. Cindy, Linda

believes she can make it all better, and just like Cindy, the issue of change is out of her control.

Lonely Linda, doesn't always start out holding onto a man like a death-defying grip, she could have been the party girl that was outgoing. However, the reason she was so outgoing was because she had to always be around people.

Now you might think, "What is wrong with wanting to be around people?" Absolutely nothing, if you are just going to meet people and have fun. But Lonely Linda is believes she's out for fun, while she's the truth is she's needy. She needs companionship all the time. She wants to find a man and use him to supplement the companionship in her life that she does not have and the attention that she craves. Lonely Linda feels lonely because she has a weak relationship with either her family or too few serious friends. In part she fears she will have no one in her life for the rest of her life.

Another problem with Linda is that she tends to smoother her boyfriend or husband with too much closeness, too much togetherness but it's not love, it's need: a need to feel appreciated; a need to feel a part of something united, a need not to feel alone, and a need to feel complete. Most often, a Linda's love interest meets her and sees a full-fledged party girl, only to have her change into this dependent woman that must spend every waking hour with him.

What's Wrong With That?

Linda is not who she pretends to be. She is living a lie and creating an illusion, (just as most of these women are). But more importantly, Linda is a "supplementer". That means that she has basic needs that she uses her new found boyfriends to supply. And unless he is the male version of Dr. Cindy (which would not be good), he will begin to feel the pressure of being so much to one person that the pressure alone will cause him to flee (yes, I did say "flee"). It generally is too much responsibility for one person within a brief amount of time. It's almost like adopting someone. They become dependent on you for everything: a phone call that says, "I miss you"; a card that says "I love you"; a date later on in the day to say, "I can't be without you and a phone call somewhere later on in the evening that says, "I thought about you after you left."

Linda intends for her boyfriends to become her mother, her father, her brother, her sister, her best friend and her lover. If she gets married, she quickly takes his family as her own, much like a surrogate family would be. Why? Because Linda has serious unresolved issues with her own family, so she attempts to replace them all with one person. Now this is not to say that Linda has no relationship with her own family; it is just not at the level or type that she would like for it to be.

Much of what Linda wants and needs could better be found by repairing her existing family ties, cultivating close friendships and looking toward herself for the additional strength she so desperately needs. However, some Lindas have strained relationships with their families for a reason: child abuse, molesting from a relative, abandonment, etc. It's not that some departures from the family aren't warranted, it's just that the feeling of loss is felt, by a Linda.

Jealous Jerri.
Jerri is jealous for one of two reasons in her relationship. She was either the mistress that took away someone else's husband/boyfriend/lover and is now afraid of him doing the same to her. Or she strongly believes that he is or was cheating, and she never really addressed it.

Jealousy is a "flagging" emotion; that means it's telling you something. It's either saying you don't trust him for some reason that could be extremely valid or that something else is wrong in your relationship. There are several women who strongly feel that their guys are cheating; this emotion could qualify as jealousy. Maybe you're jealous of the time he spends with his secretary; jealous of the time he spends with his buddies; jealous of his ex-wife, jealous of his connection and commitment with his kids. All of these thoughts make a statement: there is something missing in your relationship that you are seeing him have with someone else. And while you may call it jealousy, it may just be that you wish you had that feeling or element of closeness in the relationship that you are jealous of, in your own relationship with him.

What's Wrong With That?

Any way you look at it, something is wrong. If you suspect him of cheating, nine out of ten times he is. Cheating doesn't have to be only about sex. Even if he tells you that they are not having sex, he could still be cheating on your relationship, by not trying to have with you what he feels he has with the other person. It could be as simple as the ease of talking to his boy that you wish he had with you.

Responsible Rita.

Rita takes care of everything and everyone and in her eyes, is the only person handling business. She does everything so religiously that no one else is allowed to take part in the process. When the guy tries, for instance, to help discipline the kids, he is criticized for having a different method. When he tries to cook dinner, he is criticized for using the wrong pan. Everything is inspected with a fine tooth comb and ultimately compared to the way SHE does it. Her way is always the reference for how it should be done. In her mind, her way, is the only way.

After a while with this level of criticism, the husband/boyfriend just stops trying to help; his way is always wrong. He is never praised for making the effort. He is never praised for the good differences in his way of handling things; he is only criticized for his inability to provide a perfect mirrored version of her way, Rita's way.

Rita more than likely will read 5 books on how to have a baby, 3 books on how to raise a child and then go to parenting classes to learn how to rear a teenager. And it is not just the child, it is the house, and everything that she touches. All of which is a part of her domain and subject to comparison by her supreme all-knowing method. However, because of his inability to do anything correctly in Rita's eyes, she convinces herself that her services are required to complete all of the demands of the house and children. Ironically enough, this frees up his time to play. Secondly, her ability to make him feel inferior opens doors for other women to come in and replace her. She alone makes him vulnerable to any kind word said or item of appreciation given by anyone.

Rita will find the special words for common everyday actions or habits to make her appear to be the supreme authority on all matters of personal interest. She has deemed herself the supreme all-knowing being, the great puddle of knowledge on everything! Of course, she is not… but she believes she is. Unfortunately, this means, that anyone else's opinion is always subordinate to hers; Rita always knows what's best.

Of course, I have given you the most extreme case of Rita; but, I have seen less extreme versions of her, as well. But, the result is always the same. He gives up trying; this allows her to have dominance in her own little world and usually allows him to fall into the hands of another woman who is less controlling.

What's Wrong With That?

Rita needs to get a life! She is so wrapped up in creating her place in the world, that she's kicked everybody else out. She's so busy being a "supermom" trying to win each mini battle, that she's losing the WAR! People outside of her closely guarded world as mother and nurturer or as working woman and executive, have no value. Rita has a closed mind and needs to open up, to the thoughts of others. Her world is too narrow. She needs to allow her world to include something more than the few things that she has chosen to make her special. She has deemed these things to be her sole purpose in life, and reason for being.

Chameleon Camele.

You would think that if a guy cared about you, he would WANT you for who you are and appreciate the differences between the two of you. Right? Well, with Camele it doesn't work that way. Camele, doesn't believe in differences. She can be completely happy with who she is in one moment and the next, purposefully give-up all that she is in an effort to become all that he wants her to be.

While change is good, there is a big difference between enjoying the activities of another person and completely giving up who you are in favor of absorbing his likes, his dislikes, his hobbies, and his way of thinking. This is what Camele does.

Camele is a chameleon, forever changing her look, her likes, her aspirations, herself. She changes with each new boyfriend. Camele is one who not only believes in the Mirage method, which is the act of pretending to be someone else in order to attract someone new, but she takes it to a new extreme and actually changes who she is each time. She's not just pretending, she actually makes the attempt to change and become that different person.

I once knew a Camele who loved meat, adored the ballet, talked dirty, enjoyed playing tennis and appreciated her sales job. She met a guy who hated all of those things, and not only did she change her religion from Catholic to Judaism, but she stopped eating meat, swapped ballet seats for tickets to the African dance festivals, became very politically conservative, swapped tennis for karate and gave up sales for an indoor job at a desk.

Some change is good, but pretending to be someone you're not, can cause you to wash away the very essence of who you are. It is one thing to take up another sport that you can share or take turns going in between the African dance festivals and the ballet, but it is completely another to entirely say "I submit to become all that he wants me to be." There is nothing valiant, or selfless about it. You can say that you aren't changing who you are, but we both know that you are. Whether you verbally say it or not, actions speak louder than words and you are screaming, "I will change to make him happy!" But what about you? My concern is with what happens to Camele when he leaves, who is she then? For Camele, she "is" or "becomes" the next guy that comes along.

What's Wrong With That?
If you so easily change to become someone else, what does that say about how much you value who you were to begin with? And why isn't Camele demanding that this new guy take up some of the very hobbies and activities that SHE enjoys? It's because, Camele believes who he is, is more important than who she is. Sad isn't it?

Little girls and teenagers are generally the first ones we see to become Camele. They just want him to like them. But, why does he have the determining vote on whether this relationship will or will not work or even happen? He shouldn't, but Camele believes he does and you can believe a thing into making it true.

Little Litia.
Little Litia has not grown up. She is the female version of Juvenile Joe, and is there to please. She's the little girl who needs someone to take care of her. She requires a protector; someone to make her feel happy, pretty, confident and loved. But that's not all, Litia also fears her poor judgment. However, what she perceives as her lack of ability is really her lack of effort.

There's usually something that has happened in her life to make her not trust her choices, not believe in her ability to carry out her own responsibilities and has stopped her from fully maturing to become the woman of confidence that she could be.

What's Wrong With That?

Litia continues to be a slave to someone because she is unwilling to take a chance on herself. She would rather be a woman dependent on a man for her decisions and her future, than a woman dependent on herself for her own judgement and growth. Instead of relying on herself, it's easier for Little Litia to assume that a man (or someone else) has the better judgement, the better direction, the better forethought and therefore the better ability required to plan her life, along with his own. However, that does not mean that a woman has to be a Litia for life.

Little Litia needs to experience some small victories in her life. She needs to see that her judgement is not flawed and that her decisions are just as prone to be right or wrong as his are. Instead she views his judgement with respect and admiration, while she views her own with question and uncertainty. Little Litia could have much to contribute, if she would only allow herself. Her process of confidence requires small successes which could turn into larger ones.

Dominant Donna.

In contrast to Little Litia, Dominant Donna must always feel in control of the game (relationship). As long as she believes this, she's confident and mellow. However, the moment she doesn't, watch out because she's ready to give a show! A player of the Mating Game who has chosen to be with a Donna, knows this. So, he will do as he needs to do and "act" subservient to her. But as we all know, things are not always as they seem.

When she questions him about where or what he was doing and the truth would expose him for the user that he is, he simply responds with either, "You know I'm a man." or "It just happened." He knows that as long as he is quiet and acts as though she's got it under control, he can do whatever he wants. Because in Donna's mind, she is responsible for all things that happen to her, even events that occur through someone else. She will find some thought or act that justifies her blaming herself, and view that item as the determining factor that brought her life to this moment. So, in the end, she blames herself for his faults too.

You will see Dominant Donna on many a talk show. She is the one that is yelling, "I can't believe you did this to me! I'm not taking this shit!", while he is sitting in a chair looking quiet and innocent. He has tested her before and she has proven that she will accept lower standards of him as long as he allows her to feel that she is the dominant one and has it all under control.

The Players

When confronted with a dilemma in her relationship, Dominant Donna's brain knows that something must change. For Donna, she requires her dignity back. So, allowing her to put on her "I am Dominant Donna" act and run through her "I am in Control" routine, allows her to feel that she has shown her friends, family and the people of the world watching or otherwise, that she doesn't take that crap!

"See, I stood up for myself," she thinks. But what she is really doing is showing everybody that she has a weakness and that she has allowed some element of her life to be supplemented by this man. That's the only way he could stay. While we don't know what element it is, there is obviously some basic need that this man is satisfying in her life. We may not immediately see it by simply looking at him, but it's there. Dominant Donna needs him, not for love, but to satisfy this basic element that is essential in her life. She's a "need slave" (or need dependent) and is bound to him by the "pretty colored chains" of money, security, companionship or some other essential element required.

Donna's "look what I said, look what I did" routine is just that, a routine... that she goes through for the benefit of her own self definition each time she is embarrassed because the rest of the world has learned about her man's sexual indiscretions. She pretends to have it all in check, so that she may live to fight another day with this same no-good man.

What's Wrong With That?

Donna is pretending, off camera and on. She has allowed herself to accept mediocrity at higher levels in the game (a relationship) and settle for partial commitment by an uncommitted man. By all accounts, Donna should have it all. She is a woman who usually has it together on every other level of her life, except the relationship level. To acknowledge that her man is lying, would be to admit that she is a poor judge of character. To admit that her man is still cheating, would be to admit that she does not have the situation under control. To admit that she is being played, would be to admit that she is not in command of the matter, and these are things, she cannot do. Because she is a woman that has her "shit" together (in every other way but this) and not only would it be a painful experience to admit the truth, but it would put all of her abilities ("to judge people", "make decisions" and "to take action") into question. And that's why she won't address the reality of the situation and remains a Dominant Donna.

Beautiful Betty.

Betty looks at her beauty solely as her glowing asset. She thinks because she is "fine" (very attractive) that that will solve all of her problems. She will never be cheated on and she will always be a highly sought after commodity.

The mother in the movie "Eve's Bayou" (played by actress Lynn Whitfield) was a Beautiful

Betty. She was gorgeous, but after a person sees the pretty package it's what's inside that makes you want to keep the present (in a matter of speaking). And despite how beautiful Betty was in Eve's Bayou, her husband was still sleeping around with everybody else.

All of us have some Beautiful Betty in us. You do, if you too think, "Is the other woman prettier than me?" But, it doesn't necessarily take looks to be a the other woman. However, Beautiful Betty is still consumed by her appearance. Her self-confidence is tied completely to her appearance. And when her looks change, she becomes self-conscious. Whether it is when she gets pregnant, gains weight or gets older. She begins to question her ability to get or keep a man because in Betty's mind it was her beauty that got him in the first place.

What's Wrong With That?

It takes more than good looks to maintain a firm hold in the game (a relationship). When we allow beauty to be the only item of importance or relevance, we are setting ourselves up for a big fall. Everyone's looks will change with time and with age, some for better and some for worse. So, is that suppose to mean that when it does, you can no longer expect to have a man in your life?

No, it doesn't. However, for Betty, she is not sure, and that is disturbing. If she has a man, she is not sure if he is going to come home every night or leave her all together tomorrow, and that is not good. The problem with Betty is that she has not emphasized the right things. Sure keeping up your appearance is important, but it should not be the beginning and end all of everything that you are. A woman is comprised of so much more than her looks. She is comfort; she is companionship; she is support; she is love. But to a Betty, she is simply beauty and that is a problem that may not be realized initially in the high level game (a relationship), but is guaranteed to become one in the future.

Jolly Juliet.
Juliet thinks that life is a romance novel. She's looking for the happy ending and she finds it by ignoring the obvious issues that are facing her constantly. Whoever said "happiness is bliss" must have known Juliet. She maintains her calm, numb state through ignorance. If you told her that you saw her husband in bed with another woman, she wouldn't believe it. She is a woman that has been hand picked because she is needy and gullible. Her perceptions on reality can be easily crafted and frequently are. Most people when talking to her, sense a lack of contact with reality. This comes from being trained by her Romeo.

Juliet is without a doubt a "need slave" (need dependent) bound by pretty colored chains, just as Dominant Donna. This is what keeps her exactly where she is and stops her from progressing to where she ought to be.

What's Wrong With That?

Juliet is the perfect slave to a man. She is pretty, mentally numb and completely without the ability to question her shitty reality. She is the perfect lover, because she does everything that she is asked to do and if she has concerns that are brought into question, she believes whatever she is told by him. Players look for Juliets because they are pretty, docile and easy to manipulate and control. However, the only reason Juliet is a Juliet is because she never challenges her reality. She never truly questions the circumstances of her relationship and so in return, she just stays numb to the truth.

Really Ready Ronnie.

Ronnie is really ready and really scary. She is desperate to get married and is ready to do it by any means necessary. She is ready to use a baby to trap a man. She is ready to give him hot sex all day and every night. "Whatever it takes" is her motto. Unfortunately, Ronnie is usually the one that gets used because she is giving up something, thinking that she is going to get something else better in return, but that something else never comes. So, she ends up feeling used, she gets angry and becomes really, really scary. Guys run from the Ronnie's of the world, if they know which ones they are, not because guys don't want to get married, but because Ronnie's sole purpose of even talking to them is to get married. That is a scary thing for a guy who is just trying to hang, have some fun and meet some people.

Ronnie is an example of a woman that has become crazy with the pressures of society telling her to be married by a certain age, pregnant by another and a grandmother of three by still another. Ronnie is ready to settle for the basics and ready to trap any man who satisfies her minimum requirements by any means necessary. Her timetable is not your timetable. The position of husband is available, and all qualified applicants will be considered!

What's Wrong With That?

If Ronnie were ever to find someone acceptable, she would just scare him off. Ronnie is LONG past desperate, she is obsessed. Obsessed with the things she cannot control and with the place she wants to be. Sure, you can make yourself accessible, go to parties and functions such that you are in the mix, but you cannot guarantee that your Mr. Right will show up at the event. Ronnie needs to open her eyes to see that life is worth living and does not become completely worthless if it does not follow a set path of sequential events. Some Ronnie's get married out of a lack of options and (again) out of fear of being left with limited choices. But Ronnie is truly her own worst nightmare and enemy. Desperation can create a host of illusions and create a wealth of fears to push you into doing something that you may very well regret in a period of time equal to a jail term or a life sentence (e.g.: "…till death due us part.").

Whatever Wanda.
Wanda is taking each day, one at a time. She realizes that stories don't have to be as they are in the movies and is not judging her life by the guidelines of society. She is living it as best she can and most often is perceived as being unique. Wanda is not pressed about life and everyday matters. She realizes that she cannot force things to materialize and that even a planned strategy on how to reach motherhood or a strong game plan (a relationship) does not guarantee the occurrence of either, nor the anticipated end result: happiness. In contrast to a Jolly Juliet, if someone called a Whatever Wanda a "BITCH", Wanda would relish the moment and respond with, "Yes! I am a bitch and yes I am bitchy!" Because she is and will continue to "B –be, I –in, T –total, C –control of H -herself".

This is the attitude that I wish more women could assume. A while back, I was on a show with Black Entertainment Television and the questions from the audience included: "How do I get a man?", "Where can I find a good man?", "How do I keep a man?". The general attitude of women was, "I need to find a man". It is almost a matter of national concern or panic and absolute necessity to get a MATE! However, you don't hear men loosing sleep over this fear. A guy's attitude is: "I'm satisfied right now. If I find a woman, then maybe I will get married and add to my life, but I am happy now too." Why can't more women have that same attitude? Why can't more women say, "I am happy with me and if a nice man comes along, that would be fine too?" I'll tell you, in my opinion, it is because, we have this preconceived notion of what a life is suppose to entail. We believe that everyone is single, then they get married, then they have a family, and then they have grandchildren and then everybody lives happily ever after. But that's not the way it works all the time. Sometimes things happen out of order and sometimes items just don't happen at all.

People who epitomize the characteristics of a Whatever Wanda would be Oprah, Janet Jackson or Madonna. Madonna had fun being single. She got married. But, marriage didn't guarantee a "happily ever after story", so she got divorced and had a baby as a single mother. Also, into this category would go, Maria Carey. Maria got married, decided married life was not the move for her and got divorced and is now living happily ever after in the hot clubs of New York City.

And while Maria got married, Oprah has yet to consider marriage at all! Everyone in the world is telling Oprah to get married to her long-time boyfriend, but despite the peer pressure, she's not having it. Because she's happy NOW.

Janet Jackson, on the other hand, like Maria was married once, decided marriage didn't make her happy, so she was living life to the fullest with her long-term boyfriend of many years, and is now a free agent but will pick another one when the time is right.

And while Janet and Oprah may have millions, women of every ethnic background are still surpassing mere financially stability standards. Modern women are sustaining comfortable lifestyles all around the globe. You don't have to have millions to be financially stable; Bill Gates said it best when he said, "You may have a bank account with several million, but you can still only eat one steak at a time. There's only so much you can use and the rest is just for show." And as for the series of events regarding the progression of life, it may not happen exactly as you planned it. If it did, there would be no excitement in experiencing each day with the knowledge that all things are possible in …the game.

What's Wrong With That?

Nothing! GQ magazine had an article out years ago that was entitled, "Why Can't A Woman Be More Like A Man". Well, Wanda is more like a man. She makes her own money, she has men approaching her all the time, but she has high standards, so sometimes she says, "yes", and sometimes, she says, "no". She is not pressed about getting married. She is not concerned about having a boyfriend. In fact the times when she did commit herself to a man it wasn't that great; not because he wasn't a good person, but because unlike Chameleon Camele, she wouldn't change who she was and she realized fairly early on in the game (relationship) that they were not a good match. She wouldn't give up the things that were important to her and he wouldn't either.

A Wanda walks into a relationship without need for money, love or security. She has all of those things already. A Wanda is confident in who she is. She has her own career path, her own dreams and is looking for a man to share those things, not change them. I once had a Wanda tell me: "What do I need a man for? I don't need him to pay my bills or to buy me things. So, what do I need a man for? To WORSHIP ME! I can do everything else by myself. If he is not there to adore me, what is he there for? I can do all the rest by myself."

In the End...
So, the next time you yell, "I Got Game!" Just ask yourself, "Whose game?" "...and then make sure that that's the game that you intend to play.

Chapter 4

Creeping!

■ ■ ■

Who is the Slut?

Kelly had been sexing Trent religiously every Monday and Wednesday for a year. This would not have been an issue if Trent had not been married to Carol. The sad fact is, Carol knew Kelly. She just didn't know that Kelly was Trent's extra little somethin', somethin' on the side. My question to you is this: "If Carol knows Kelly, why is it a surprise to her that Kelly and Trent are creeping?"

When most women think of a play thing, a mistress or the other woman, they think of "the hoochie from the bar that laid up with my [their] man". But, it's much deeper than that. Women can be the most deceitful creatures. They can be the best of friends within one breath, and become the worst of enemies within the next. Life is fine and everyone is a "sista" until a fine, good-looking man walks into the picture. Then within an instant, and as if by magic, girlfriend don't know you. However, men don't play that same game between men.

Two men can knowingly or unknowingly find out they slept with the same woman, call her a "ho", drop her and still be the best of friends. Women do it in reverse. Women will start out being the best of friends, drop the girlfriend, get called or call someone a "ho", then sleep with the man.

So, who is the slut? She is your best friend, your cousin, your sister, and sometimes even your mother. She is anyone. No position in or outside of the family is sacred.

So, why was Carol surprised to learn that her husband's play thing was Kelly? Because Carol and Kelly went to school together, grew up together and Kelly was Carol's Bride's Maid at her wedding to Trent. Kelly was closer to her than a sister or Carol's mother. Kelly was the only family she had for a good piece of her life and because of that confidence, Carol felt she could tell Kelly everything and anything, and Carol did. Carol told Kelly so much information that she single-handedly prepared Kelly to be the perfect side fling that Trent was looking for. Carol had helped Kelly become the person that Trent had tried to make Carol into.

However, unlike Carol, Kelly progressed at this transformation without discussion and without resistance. And just like the song, "You're My Little Secret," the fact that Carol didn't know about Trent and her really turned Kelly on sexually.

Female Snaring Methods
"I keep my friends close and my enemies closer..."
--Anonymous

The snaring methods that women use against other women are really treacherous. It's a sad thing to know that your best friend can become your worst nightmare. So, how do women play each other to take men?

The Best Friend from Hell.
This to me is the worst of all prospects, because this is a person you trusted so completely. We all know how this works. She may not start out with the intention of stealing your guy, but it sure ended up that way. This is the person you would suspect last and by then it's too late, the damage is

done. And she's the woman that far too many songs have been written about.

How does it Work? She is of course your best girlfriend, so you tell her everything. All the good and the bad intimate details of your game (relationship). So, now you have given her the ability to step right into the player's circle with everything he wants and understanding everything that he needs.

How do you protect against this? It's simple. Do NOT tell your girlfriends the intimate details of your relationship. You can talk to them to GET information, but do not GIVE intimate information. For instance, you could ask what is the best lingerie out right now or ask if they know of some new restaurant to go to. But do NOT tell them the blow by blow details of your intimate ups and downs. That only serves to wet their appetite for more, and gives them the potential power to move in, even if it isn't right at that moment.

If you are having problems and need someone to talk to; talk to your boyfriend or husband. He is the one that you need to work it out with and he is the only one that can truly provide you with the answers to the questions you may have about what's wrong. Everybody else is just guessing.

Partners in Crime.
This is another method of deceit. Unlike The Best Friend from Hell, your competition in this

method is known to you as the competition. The only difference is that you both agree to a temporary truce in order to get to the heart of the matter and resolve the issue. However, just like the previous method, girlfriend is still working as your competition, only now it's a covert operation; she's undercover. The only question is whose covers and in whose bed?

How does it Work? You meet your boyfriend's other girlfriend. And just like in Brandy and Monica song, "The Boy is Mine", you both conspire to show him up together. Well, in the "Partners in Crime" version of that video, one of the two women would be coming over to collect information. However, what we see is that one of the two women is only giving information about how they were great together, whereas the other woman feels comfortable and free to tell everything: good and bad (just as in The Best Friend from Hell).

After both women show him up (together) in the doorway, the one girlfriend who has been collecting the information from the other woman, then confronts the boyfriend in an attempt to show how loyal she was and displays how the other woman betrayed his trust by telling everything. She further goes onto agree to take him back if he will change his ways. (She's playing that Dominant Donna role.) The funny thing about this, however, is that the woman who calls herself winning the game by going back and taking boyfriend on her "own terms" has really fallen victim to the "winner's curse" (to win at any cost, only to discover that by winning you have actually lost). Ironically, now the girlfriend who calls herself the winner because she has the boyfriend, now has NO playing cards or power. She has shown boyfriend that she will stay at any cost. So now, he will go out and be even more daring or more adventurous in finding women. Because she has proven that despite what he does and is CAUGHT doing, she is NOT going anywhere. Therefore, there's no threat. Her trump card is gone, and he continues to have fun playing as a free agent (dating other women).

Queen Bee.
    While Beautiful Betty believes that beauty is the element required to get a man for life, the Queen Bee believes that GOOD SEX is the way to a man's heart. And while the Queen Bee is correct in believing that men do want SEX, she is incorrect in believing that a strong sexual performance will continue to keep him around. Sadly enough, a man's length of stay in the Queen Bee's life is equal to the length of time required by him to pull his pants both DOWN plus UP. A Queen Bee is on a man's Permanent Booty Call List. Usually, the Queen Bee attempts to adapt the same "I-don't-give-a-damn-about-sex" attitude that men have, but it's a mistake. A Queen Bee typically ends up getting used basically because she has set the stage for herself to be used. She's made no demands; she is sex without commitment. Or so she says. She has asked for nothing therefore she gets nothing in return.

This is how it Works: The Queen Bee is usually a woman who is attempting to snare a man. She believes that sex is the essential ingredient in a relationship so she will give it to him; however he wants it, whenever he wants it, in whatever manner or place that he wants it. She will act as though she is the only woman in the world that can provide this man with coochie; she believes she has special sexual skills or coochie talents. So, she tries harder and harder to please him sexually. She is trying to be all that he sexually wants in a woman. She doesn't realize that you can't trap a man with sex, if he doesn't want to be trapped. All of which he enjoys regardless and then he will find 2, 3 or 4 more "Queen Bees" just like her. willing to please. This is what most guys call… "Coochie Heaven"!!

Now, when one Queen Bee finds out she has one or more rivals, you might think that the game is up, right? Wrong! Queen Bees believe that no one can give coochie like they can give coochie. So, they all start to participate in a sex competition that I sometimes refer to as a Coochie Competition. Everyone is trying to top the others coochie score in every event.

Each woman tries to out-sex the other. Of course, the guy is loving it, because he doesn't really want a relationship with any of them anyway; he's just enjoying the sex! And now to be the object of a sex competition is too good to be true.

Now eventually, one or two of the women might wake up after a few weeks or months of this, because their intent has been to win the Coochie Competition. But he doesn't want to end it, so every time they ask boyfriend to make a decision, he just uses a method of lying. So, one or two women finally realize that he has no intention of stopping the Coochie Competition, and they leave. But that is really of little concern to him. He can always find a couple more Queen Bees to take the available openings.

Now, I'm sure you would think that the story ends there, but it doesn't. He will have fun with his new found flavors of the month in his on-going sex competition and sooner or later he will get bored with one or decide that he wants to return to the previous flavor of the month that left. Now, I'm sure that you probably think that no self-respecting woman would return to the Coochie Competition, but ...oh, you are wrong.

Boyfriend is not stupid; he is a master of manipulation and understands these women better than they understand themselves. He realizes that the only reason the two that left did so, was because he wouldn't make a decision and pick one. So, he will wait a while after he has had his fun with a couple of the others and let the new ones depart, then he will call up each of the two girlfriends that left and, of course, tell them that what happened before is all over and that he has left the others. Leaving them to believe that they have both emerged victoriously as his only pick or his woman of choice.

Now, if you have scanned the chapter on lying, you will know by now that people believe what they want to believe, and if she misses the sex or his companionship or the fun and excitement that they use to have and she has not been able to find an adequate replacement for him, she WILL go back!

I have seen the most intelligent woman do this. So, don't think that a woman would have to be stupid or ignorant, in order to unknowingly put herself back in the exact same position that she left. No, that's not required. She just needs to be a bit lonely and needy for something in her life that she believes he can provide.

Jail Bait Mate.
How many times have we thought to ourselves: "It's only the baby-sitter."; "It's only a teenager."; "She's only a child." As if to say, that the slightest possibility that the baby-sitter could sex your husband up and take your place is both obscene and remote. Yet, how many well-known people can claim to have had their husbands or boyfriends taken away by a previously known minor? How could this happen?

Well, the first line of broken defense is that women like to talk. They talk when they are happy and they talk when they are sad and upset. The problem is that they are most always talking to the wrong person. They will tell their most intimate secrets and problems to anyone and everyone who they do not perceive as a threat. The problem with that is that everyone can be a threat, perceived or otherwise.

Now, how many well-known people have openly confessed to leaving their wives for the baby-sitter, or a soon to be teenaged star. I can think of at least four immediately. One of which (previously a baby-sitter, now a second wife) was said to have been the person this previous couple wholeheartedly named their last born child after. And his original wife was absolutely Gorgeous (with a capital "G"). Obviously looks had very little to do with it because the baby-sitter was extremely plain; hell, that girl was so young, she hadn't even fully developed her breasts!

I can think of two Jail Bait Mates, a manager for a pre-teen Canadian/French singer. and the other managed a teen skater. Both girls (the skater and the singer) were only 10 or 13 (respectively) when these men starting traveling around the country with them to help promote their careers.

Can you imagine being one of the original wives? You would not have thought anything of your husband traveling around the country with a 10 or 13 year old girl. Imagine their surprise to later be told: "I'm leaving you for a now 17 or 18 year old woman that I have now formed a 6 year relationship with." Can you feel the horror?

Creeping!

These girls are students of the school of MIT (Mistress In Training School). Somewhere along the way they've been taught to believe that this type of behavior is alright. Whether that approval has come from their parents, their friends or the men that have approached them, the school motto remains the same "Allegiance to None."

On the other side of the MIT School, I've met mothers who willingly prostitute their daughters out to the highest bidder. These girls learn to accept it in exchange for what they perceive to be a better way of life. It's difficult for a young girl with limited experience to understand why this is hurtful to them when they only see the positives of their relationships with older men. I try to explain it like this:

Let's imagine that you own one very valuable piece of furniture, that's been valued at close to a $100,000. Unfortunately, it's the only thing of real value that you have. You live in a run down apartment, your bank account has nothing but bounced checks and you haven't bought a new outfit in 3 years. One day someone comes to your door and sees the valuable antique and likes it very much. You don't want to permanently sell it, because it's all that you have. So, this person offers to rent it for $200. Being that you don't have anything, this $200 sounds GREAT! In fact it sounds like a lot of money to someone who has none. So, you jump at the chance, but this person says, "Wait a minute. In exchange for this money, I must be permitted to do anything to this antique that I want." You agree.

The next day, your beautiful antique is returned. You immediately notice that it has some scratches on it. But no matter, you are $200 richer!

This same person then comes back the following day with the same offer. You agree to the transaction again. The antique is brought back and this time you notice that one of the legs is slightly damaged, but no matter because you are again $200 richer than you were the day before.

This same person continues with this offer for 6 months, 3 times every week. You have now grossed over $14,400!! This is too good to be true! As a result of your new found wealth, you have been able to pay your rent, buy some nice pieces of furniture, and even managed to buy a few nice pieces of clothing. Things couldn't be better. But, you notice that your antique doesn't look as good as it use to. Although you never really paid it much attention anyway. It was just an old piece of furniture that sat in the corner doing nothing. Still you can't help but notice that it's not the same; the antique is kind of dented up now. But it's old and old things have dents and are less than perfect. Right?

When you look a little closer, you notice that one leg is completely broken off and nailed back on. There are a few water stains, the top isn't as shiny and it doesn't have a glowy surface anymore. So, you think, "I've got a few extra dollars, maybe I should check out getting these small things fixed". I mean you are $14,400 dollars richer than you were 6 months ago.

So you find a place and take it in to get it repaired. The day you take it in, the guy that can fix the piece happens to be in. You introduce yourself, tell him how this piece of furniture use to sit in the corner but now from use you need to get it repaired. You ask the man, "Can you repair it?"

"Oh, sure!" he replies. He continues, "of course it won't have the same value as it did"

You're puzzled, "Value, what do you mean by value?"

"Well, you know how these things are relative to wear and tear...."

"No, I don't. What are you talking about?"

"Well, we appraise pieces like this all the time."

"Appraise? Well, what would you appraise this piece at?"

"Well, this is a very nice piece. In perfect condition, I would say it would be worth no less than....say $100,000."

"Right." you know that, so you confirm it by answering, "Correct, this piece is worth $100,000?"

"Well, no. That's not what I said."

"Of course that's what you said! I heard you say it. I was standing right hear when I heard you say...$100,000!"

"No, I said it would be worth $100,000 in perfect condition."

"Okay...well. You can't go down much from $100,000. I mean it's still the same piece. Right?"

"Oh, sure!"

You begin to become relieved.

He continues. "It's the same piece physically, but in the eyes of the market we are talking a whole 'nother ball game here."

You're confused, "What?"

"Yep. In the marketplace that's a whole different story."

"So, what are you trying to tell me?" You become a bit overly anxious, "How much is it worth?"

"Before, in excellent condition, $100,000. Now, with all of these scratches, dents and broken leg...hmmm, even after repairs I would have to say it wouldn't be valued at slightly more than $10,000."

You can't believe this.

You might have thought the $200 was a lot of money when it was put into your hands, but now you discover that you traded $90,000 in value for $14,400. You were ROBBED!!!

That's what you do with yourself when you date men solely for money. I know you're thinking, that you're not worth $100,000. You are right. You're monetary value is much higher. If you think of every dollar spent on you as part of the investment made in you; it's much higher.

When you were born, hospital cost were probably about $20,000. The cost of clothing and food every year at it's lowest figure, is about $15,000.Multiplying this figure alone for a 13 year old person brings the total value to $210,000 (and that is a LOW figure). We haven't added the value of your parent's time and effort in raising you, the cost of college, etc. The figure gets higher and higher. So, I say all of this to say what? "Don't devalue and sell yourself short.

The Other One-Man.

Remember, everyone could be or become the other woman. Now, I'm not trying to make you paranoid; I'm just trying to keep you alert. You might be thinking, "Now Anita is tripping! Hell, my gay hairdresser is not a threat to me." But is he?

There are several gay men that love to turn out straight men. Secondly, with homosexuality only recently becoming an item of remote acceptance, their are still many gay men, living a straight life out of fear of ridicule.

Do you remember the local song that quickly became a national surprise hit on the song and dance charts called "Bill"? Oh, yes, I think you do. It was a song about a man who was a close friend to both a woman and her husband. However, soon the woman in the song discovered that this person her husband had been having an affair with was named "Bill". Oh, yes, and there were far too many women around the country requesting that song for it not to have hit a nerve of familiarity. So, let me correct you if you just thought that some people were 100% safe; ... because no one is.

I'm "Ready"!

Girlfriends and wives are puzzled by a reoccurring situation. They want to know, "Why is my boyfriend or husband sleeping with another woman, when she is not prettier, younger, thinner or smarter than me?" What does the other woman have that you don't?" That is a question that has many layers of answers, one of which is that the other woman is "ready": ready for sex, ready for fun, ready to try new things, ready to listen, and just plain ready!

On one of my radio shows, I brought on two sex experts. You guessed it... "adult" film stars! You are probably thinking, "Anita! Why would you have asked porn stars about sex?"

Come on now! When you ask the question, you immediately hear the answer. If you have a question about teeth, you don't go to someone who has never worked with teeth. You go to someone who works with teeth on a regular basis!

Well, the same is true, in my mind, about sex. If you have a question about sex, who are you going to go to for the answers? Some person who can theoretically explain it to you? Or someone who works with the equipment on a regular basis?

You got it! My vote goes to the person that deals with the various aspects of sex every day. To me, this person has the same credibility as a dentist and for the same reason. So, with all of that said, when we began talking about this very subject of men cheating on their beautiful wives, these two film stars (and sexual fantasy providers) said to me: "The men that come to me have shown me pictures of their wives and these women are gorgeous! I've asked, 'Why are you with me?'"

The answer they give, she said, is "Variety!" She provides variety without making judgments about what is appropriate or socially acceptable. The point here is that maybe more women need to be a little more open to trying new things. I would, of course, say the same to men. The hope is that a sexual relationship will also take on the aspect of give and take, such that both people can be satisfied.

On that note, a group of men were asked, "Are you satisfied with your sex life?" Within this group, 58% said that they were not. Indirectly, that means to me that 58% of the women involved with these men could be experiencing BETTER sex through trying new experiences.

The mistress, other woman or other one-man, on the other hand, is ready to cater to a man's every whim or request, sexual or otherwise. But, then again, it's easy to be "ready" when you don't have to deal with the constant pressures of everyday life: the children, the job, the household, and so on.

In a poll that was done, men were asked: "What are the biggest deterrents to your feeling sexy and romantic?" Of all the answers that were given, almost all of them were related to the pressures of every day life.

One man said it best: "My girlfriend always wants to talk about the household bills. When I come home from work, my girlfriend wants to tell me about every little detail that happened to her at work or nag me about when I'm going to take out the trash or complete some other household thing.

Personally, I don't care to know every solitary detail of her day and I don't like being nagged about picking up a dish from the dinner table when I've just spent 10 hours at work catering to my boss's every request and listening to him constantly reminds me about what I need to get done."

A mistress (or a play thing) doesn't have these kinds of discussions, nor does she make these types of demands. She is ready at all times. She is a separate entity from his home life, so she can't possibly remind him of what he should have done or what needs to be done. Think about it. It doesn't have to be that way. A slight change (here and there) and you can provide the same type of benefit that he (or she) is missing.

Don't Worry Be Happy

Imagine: A woman sits down to talk to her boyfriend or husband, right after he walks through the door. She immediately starts to bring him up to date with the events of her day. He sits quietly. She then begins talking about the bills and discussing which ones to pay. Around that time, their 3-year-old son runs into the room and starts circling a chair. Dad calls out to his son to calm down. She continues on and reminds him that they have a dinner date with another couple on the weekend.

So, what does a mistress have that a wife or a girlfriend doesn't? The answer is time and the absence of complexity. Time with her is simple and limited. He can't discuss bills with her, because they share no bills. He may pay some of hers, but they don't share them. He can't discuss group date plans, because he has to be careful about where the two of them are seen. They have to effectively use their time, because they don't have unlimited amounts of it. Therefore, the time they do have together is precious. When they're together, they are both of the same mind in knowing what they're going to do; they are going to enjoy each other.

This lack of time indirectly results in a higher level of concentrated pleasure. Think about that for a moment. If you got a free ticket to Hawaii and the only condition was that you could only spend 12 hours on the island then return home, you're not going to wait until tomorrow to do all the fun things you want to do. You're going to make some determinations and start having fun the moment you get there.

If you really think about it, the time that a married or serious couple have together could be perceived in the same manner as a short Hawaii trip or the 2-hour fling of pleasure in a hotel room. It's all a matter of perception and actively rearranging the events of the day. With a little bit of thought and a touch of creativity, any woman could induce a similar type of excitement.

So, lets talk about what you need to work your magic.

Tools Of The Trade

Sex, money, trust and communication are the main tools of manipulation used in the Mating Game. Whether we use one or the other, everyone has their desired weapon of choice. We've discussed "sex", now let's talk about the other tools.

Money.
"God, bless the child whose got his own..."
--Billy Holiday

Money does for a man, what cosmetics do for a woman. The more he's got the more attractive he is. You can take a guy who's not really stunningly attractive, put him next to a Mercedes and improve his looks by ten fold! However, Some guys need more help than others. So, they walk around with a pocket full of money. To these men, women say: "It will take more than that." So, he tells everyone through casual conversation: "I got a Mercedes in the parking lot, a penthouse apartment, and if your nice to me, I'll take you on my yacht." Suddenly, he has become irresistible! But not every woman is like that.

Money can only be used against you, if you allow it to. A decision of that nature is made without your permission an approval. However, sometimes that permission is given submissively through lack of action or through your inability to say, "no".

Trust.

What relationship is complete without trust? We are told that you must have trust in a relationship or you have nothing. This "trust" is a double edged sword that cuts like a knife both ways.

You tell your guy that your relationship must be based on trust and the cheating man feels, he is home free. Why? Because, if you trust him, then you will believe the stories he will tell you. You will not question why he has been out at all hours of the night and you will not question any female who calls, while you are there. Why? Because you trust him. So, he knows that you would not confront any one of his many women, because it would display a lack of trust on your part and he knows that you want to trust him and will make every effort to allow him to correct any perceived wrong, because you trust that he will do, "What is right?"

Trust is the ultimate weapon. Women who disagree believe that they must know a guy's every move, must watch him like a dog, must question his every thought and decision. But to do that would be an intrusion on your own life. He would be taking away from your energy. It takes a lot of work to spy on someone. To do it on a continuous basis is time consuming. Few women have enough hours in the day to run and keep track of their own lives, let alone keep tabs on a man's life at all hours of the day and night. In the end, the bottom line of decision becomes: trust but verify! Do not trust blindly. Question everything that you feel requires a question. If he has nothing to hide, then there should be no problem in asking the questions. To trust blindly is to turn your back, while someone rudely stabs you with the very sword (called trust) that you gave them. But if you have to question his every move, every hour of every day, then you don't have trust. In fact, something has happened to damage your trust. And if he has and has not proven to you that he can again be trusted, then you need to ask yourself, "Is this the way I want to live my life?"

Communication

Communication is one of the more powerful tools. How else could a liar give you the perfect response, unless you told him/her what you wanted to hear first? A cheating man will use several approaches to keep you docile and on guard. I call these the "*control statements*".

Control statements are generally statements that you initially can't do anything about. They are items that require long-term planning or effort for change. So much so, that if you ever did attempt to do something about it, by the time you made the statement untrue, he would have another problem to bring your mental image of yourself into question again. These statements put you immediately on the defensive or make you cave in with a feeling of having already been defeated, like...

1. You're too Fat!

So, why is he with you? I did a show about women who had given birth to a child and still hadn't lost all of the weight gained from having had the baby. To hear the way these men talked about these women was amazing. One guy actually said, "Yep, I call her fat, bitch, ho, because I feel she needs some encouragement." I never forgot that, because it was just so unbelievably brutal.

Another woman actually sat on the stage and told the world that she could become bulimic (a very serious eating disorder that has a very high death rate). I don't know how her husband did it, but he somehow blocked the sound waves from his wife. While she was telling the world that she could acquire an eating disorder and die, her husband heard nothing. Immediately, after her statement, her husband again called her fat! No matter how many times I see it, I am still frequently amazed by the men that constantly tease their women about being bigger than they would like and yet many of these men weigh more than Fat Albert (the cartoon character) themselves! One woman, came out first and told us all about how her husband said she had no neck. She was about a size 10. Then her husband came on stage and it was obvious that he had to go to the Big & Tall Men's Store, because he was a large man. One audience member asked him if he served as a stand in for Eddie Murphy in the movie "The Nutty Professor"; ...that's how big he was.

You may think that a strong woman can handle nasty comments like that, but even a strong woman can get weak. The women I saw up on the stage were not weak women. They really were not.

But the negative repetition of their boyfriend's and husband's consistent demeaning comments was wearing them down, and you could see it.

2. You're too Skinny!

You would think that if you are anything but overweight, you would have it made. But that's not true. Anything other than his perception of perfection will be enough to cause you problems. And if it wasn't too much weight or too little weight, believe me, it would be something else: you're too needy; you're too whiney; you're too...(something).

One woman came out before her makeover and told everyone that her boyfriend constantly complained about how she didn't have any butt or any breasts. So, again I asked...my original question, "If it's that bad; why is he with her?" The answer is that making these statements is not about helping her become better in her appearance, it's all about knocking her confidence down so that he can better control her. Women that are constantly knocked down will cater to a man's every whim better in an effort to prove herself worthy of his love. It's an indirect way of creating or maintaining a Jolly Juliet.

3. You're Plain.

Again. "So, why is he with her?" I've yet to meet a make-up artist who couldn't solve this problem. Some of the most beautiful women in the world are really rather plain without their make-up too. In fact, I have heard stories about two of the Super Models that threatened to sue a couple of photographers if they took pictures of them without their make-up on.

However, someone who feels as though she is plain is probably not one who goes to the beautician for a haircut or treats herself to a new outfit or even gets her nails and make-up done that often. In fact, she is usually a beauty in disguise who has never quite tried to polish and refine what she has always had.

3. You're just all into her business because, you don't HAVE a man!
This is the classic response that every man will use when he has run out of excuses or things to say to some woman who is trying to rescue a Juliet or a Rebound Babe from her captor. When someone is attacking you, what would you do?

    A. Continue to address the topic being discussed which is you and how you treat your wife, or...

    B. Attempt to quickly get off the topic at hand by saying something negative about someone else that instead puts them on the defensive?

Obviously, men do "B". They will put you on the defensive and lead you into a trap of talking about you, which then leaves you yelling in defense of yourself. Completely distracted by the new topic, you abandon discussion about him, in pursuit of defending your own honor. This suits him just fine, because you have allowed yourself to be led down the path he wanted, away from HIM. Now you are defending yourself, when that was NOT suppose to be the item of discussion on your agenda. It was suppose to be him. And his wife, thinks, "Well, I guess, it's true. At least I have a man." But with a man like that, you're better off with nothing.

4. Why can't you look like her?
You can never look exactly like someone else and truly if you could, why would you want too? But again, this is a way of knocking you down. You are not this other woman, therefore, in reality you could never look like her or someone else. Now this is different from getting your hair cut to be "similar" to that of a person in a magazine, or getting a skirt "like" a girl he saw walking down the street. We are talking about him wanting you to be someone else.

Hell, if he wants her then he needs to just go get that woman now, because for you to attempt to be anybody other than who you are would be insane; yet still some women put themselves through the torture of trying, an act that can only end in defeat.

Someone who demands that you become someone else, is obviously not interested in you, nor does he care about you. When control statements like these are used to keep you in check, that should be your signal to start reviewing your other options, like LEAVING. It's a signal that this game plan (relationship) "as it is" is not going to work.

Chapter 5

The Rules

...of The Mating Game

■ ■ ■

Playing by the Rules

In the Mating Game, like any other game, the winner is always the one who understands the rules better. However, with so many people playing to win, the rules often change. The trick is to remember the rules that govern The Mating Game in principle and create your own rules for everyone else to play by, ...if they want to play with you.

Through the course of this book, we will discuss in detail several items that are summarized within this chapter and several items that are not. However, these are the basic rules of The Mating Game.

Rule #1:
Men can only think with one head at a time.

Explanation:
It may be crude, but we all know it's true. A man in bed telling a woman that he loves her, can't be held responsible for that statement later. Because, his little head was already in use. Therefore, a man who pulls up to you at first sight and tells you that he thinks the two of you could have a long and lasting relationship, right after the two of you go kick it (have sex) in his apartment, isn't talking with his big head. The little head is talking to you.

I do know that there will be several men, who will proudly proclaim that their big head is not attached to their necks but is instead in their pants, and I would have to confirm that for those men, who confess it, that statement would be true. Because, if they are that proud of having a big head in their pants, they are correct. Their big head is in their pants and their little head is at the other end attached to their neck with an equally smaller brain.

Rule #2:
No woman, only wants sex.

Explanation:
    Women have tried many tactics to win The Mating Game, one of which is to play by the Players' Rules (Player Pete's Rules), which generally ends up being HIS rules. Men love that because it means, let's get nasty now and I'll see ya later. Despite, how any woman wants to present herself in the Mating Games, a woman cannot change the way she operates. Every woman consciously makes a decision, takes into consideration the impact on her heart and then moves toward the option of sex. Even the loosest woman still operates in the same manner. Whether her logic is:

- He could pay my bills, bills, bills.
- He would satisfy my sexually appetite tonight.
- He could make someone else very jealous, or
- He could buy me some nice jewelry and things.

A woman is, has and will always take into consideration, her game plan. It may not be completely credible or even a great plan, but you can bet money that she has engaged the brain in the activity of thought prior to deciding to get down and dirty. Men, on the other hand, are the opposite. They act now, think later, and then look for forgiveness, immediately after someone says, "Didn't you think before you did it!" The honest answer should be "Yes. I was thinking with my little head." Women who try to operate this way will always get hurt and end up misleading others (along with themselves), because women just don't function that way. Women who attempt to operate like a man, end up selling themselves short because they cheat themselves out of getting what they keep telling themselves they don't want.

Rule #3:
Men are creatures of habit and repetition.

Explanation:

Despite our desire to believe that men are so very difficult to understand, they are not. Men are primarily creatures of habit. A man that leaves the cap off the toothpaste before you met him, is going to leave the cap off the toothpaste after you meet him. A man that mistreated his last girlfriend, is more than likely, going to mistreat his next one too. It's not that difficult. A woman who dates a man who speaks poorly of his last girlfriend, will probably speak poorly of his current one when her time comes to breakup.

It's actually to a woman's advantage really. If you open your eyes to see what he is, you know what he was and realize what he shall be. Men are what they are. Now, that's not to say that an old dog can't learn a few new tricks, but it is to say that "what you see, is what you get".

Conversely, women that don't try to change their men, generally tend to be the women that men appreciate more. And who wouldn't? Women that don't try to change their men are indirectly saying: I like you just the way you are, and who couldn't appreciate that?

Rule #4:
Women are creatures of emotion.

Explanation:

While men tend to operate on a more simplistic plane. Women convert all situations to an emotional one: attack, breach or concern. For instance: If she gets upset about his not taking out the trash, it's not about the trash. She's upset because he is not SHARING the responsibilities; he is not RESPECTING her request; she believes that he is belittling HER VALUE (by thinking that she can take out the trash). You see how it works. Let's do another one.

Your girlfriend decides to make you dinner. She spends a couple of hours making a fancy fish dish that includes a cream sauce. You sit down to eat and start picking around the sauce eating the fish only. When she asks you why you aren't eating the sauce, you then tell her that you are allergic to milk. She is now upset. However, she is not upset about the sauce. She is upset because you didn't FEEL that your RELATIONSHIP was important enough to SHARE the simple fact that you are allergic to milk. She's concerned that your inability to

COMMUNICATE displays a lack of DEVELOPMENT in your RELATIONSHIP, which leads her to question your CLOSENESS with her.

The next time you fail to complete a task, if you look for the emotional connection to her in the item and convey that information to her before she has an opportunity to confront you by being upset, I guarantee you she will start believing: "My man, he understands me SO WELL!"

Rule #5:
Women are easily manipulated by words.

Explanation:
To their detriment, women are too forgiving. For the many reasons discussed in this book and more, women will take a kind word and build a life on it. They hear the words "I do" at the alter and believe that forever "he will". In the world of reality, words run thin, and everyone can promise the moon, while few will actually deliver it. In reality, "I'm sorry" doesn't necessarily mean "I'm sorry"; and "I will never cheat on you again," doesn't necessarily mean that he "...will never cheat on you again". It's like Chris Rock said: "A man is only as faithful as his options..."

Actions on the other hand, speak louder and make a stronger statement of commitment to the verbal word. A person can say he loves you, but does he make you FEEL loved? A man can say you're important, but does he make you FEEL important? I personally will take an action over a word any day, but that's just me.

Rule #6:
Emotional baggage, which are unresolved relationship issues, will haunt you until you mentally confront them, openly challenge them and finally convert them to a life experience which can be stored as wisdom.

Explanation:
No one is perfect. Everyone has had some experience that has been negative and hopefully everyone has had an experience or two that can be labeled as positive. The goal in playing the Mating Game is not to play it perfectly, but to learn with each Game experience how to play it better. Too many of us, sit for days depressed about the fact that a relationship didn't work out, instead of reflecting on the positive time experienced and looking forward to the next Mating Game adventure!

Instead, we concentrate of the negative: "He didn't like me." "She thought that I was boring." "He said I was too possessive." Well, your answers to these statements respectfully should be: who cares; I'm going to have fun anyway, and I'll see about letting go more. When you carry the results of a previous Mating Game experience in your head as a mark against you, it becomes a secret item that no one can talk about. These items must remain in a deep, dark closet. These things in the closet can keep you from having fun and stop you from moving forward in the next round of the Mating Game. If you instead chose to confront the issue, and through mental consideration or discussion with friends convert it to a learning experience then you will be one up for a positive experience on your next go round on the Mating Game.

Rule #7:
Experiences will repeat themselves until the lessons are learned.

Explanation:
There are people who constantly find themselves in the same situation over and over again and wonder why. For instance:

- Your friend down at the spa keeps dating these guys that are no good for her.

- Your friend down the street finds herself constantly breaking-up with guys.

- The guy you know at work keeps going back to his ex-wife.

Why? The reason is actually not that difficult. There is a lesson or understanding that you are ignoring with each recurring experience and you are constantly finding your way back to the same situation or experience because you cannot move forward until you recognize why the experience needs to change and extract the lesson. For instance:

- Your friend down at the spa that keeps making poor choices in men does so, may because she doesn't see what characteristics or elements make those men poor choices. Despite how many times you pull a person out of a bad game (relationship), until they understand what the items are that made that relationship bad, they will continue to make the mistake of looking for the same wrong elements in a man again, be it through going back to the old one or finding a replacement that will be just as bad.

- Your friend down the street who keeps breaking up with guys, may be indirectly sabotaging her own relationships because she doesn't want to be in them or maybe it's because she needs to spend some time with herself and that is the one thing she has avoided doing: cultivating a relationship with self.

- The guy you know at work who keeps going back to his wife, may be doing that because he wants to be with her but he hasn't addressed an important item that continues to keep them apart or maybe he doesn't want to be with her and is more afraid of being alone than of challenging the unknown and for finding someone new. As a result, he keeps going back to his wife (his Rebound Babe) who presents a warm and cozy place, but it continues to be less than he wants and therefore, he finds himself in conflict creating a yo-yo effect: leaving, reuniting, leaving, reuniting, and leaving.

Oddly enough, we all know the answers for our own problems, we just avoid them. Repetition in life experience is an indirect way of forcing us to confront these items, and that's why we continue to repeat the same mistakes and find ourselves making the same poor decision and choices. The item hasn't been converted to wisdom.

Rule #8:
What you do onto others is immediately done onto you.

Explanation:
I think we all know that I didn't come up with this one. It came from a more popular book called the Bible, and although I'm not trying to be religious, the statement appears to be a simple fact of truth.

Women who say, "I'm just using him for sex," were also being used for sex. Just as there are women who spend time with men because they have money to buy them pretty things; conversely, men stay with those women until they no longer want to buy THEM... Most all of these men with the dollar bills (Mr. Dollar Bill) could only be with these women because they have money and these men know this. Because the moment he becomes a dollar short, a woman will fire his ass and move on to the next Dollar Bill. So, it's better to know that whatever you think you are getting away with by doing to someone else, you are actually doing right back to yourself..

Rule #9:
Find value and joy in what you have, instead of what you wish you had.

Explanation:
    I know you've heard the story of the dog that had a bone, went across the bridge and saw his reflection in the water. He thought the reflection was another dog with a bone and being greedy, he decided he was going to have his bone and the other dog's too. So, when he opened his mouth his bone fell out into the water and then he had none. Well, that's the thought I'm trying to get too when I say be happy with what you've got.

    You don't really value what you have until you've lost it and then you realize that what you had, DID have value after all. There's nothing wrong with wanting more, but if the dog in the story had valued what he had, he would have paused for a moment to put down his bone before he attempted to reach for the second one.

Rule #10:
Thoughts are things.

Explanation:
How you think of yourself is actually the pre-requisite to building yourself. If I asked you how you see yourself, your answer would probably illustrate you as you are currently. The way we think of ourselves and how we perceive our lives does a lot to shape who we are and what we actually look like. Negative thoughts can help bring those ideas into reality.

They say that every invention was conceived as a thought first before it came into reality to be. If that's true, then human beings are being built and rebuilt everyday through our thoughts and perceptions of ourselves and others. So, be careful of the thoughts you allow into your head from others, because thoughts are real things too.

Rule #11:
Allowing exceptions to the rules set precedents for recurring offenses.

Explanation:
A girlfriend of mine, Terry, was dating a guy who kept cheating on her. When I asked her when she was going to put her foot down she said: "I did! I told him he better not bring those hoochie mammas in my house and in my bed!"

I asked her, "So, where is he?"

"Out with those hootchie mammas."

"...and you find this acceptable, Terry?"

"What am I suppose to do? I can't be trailing around after him!"

When I first met my Terry, she told me that she was NEVER going to let this man cheat on her like he had with his other girlfriend. About a month later, after she had caught him cheating, she said she was giving him another chance. He said he wasn't going to cheat on her anymore. Six months later, not only is he still cheating with great known frequency, but he had actually slept with another woman in her bed. So, with each provision, she had allowed her stands to go from "He will never cheat on me," to "He will never cheat on me in my BED, again." That leaves a lot of room for cheating...

The point being that each time she gave him another chance, he continued to chew away at what was unacceptable until she had been trained to accept what he gave her. Therefore, I say "exceptions create reoccurring offenses in the Mating Game."

Rule #12:
Negotiations take place before marriage, not after.

Explanation:
In the course of this book several subjects will and have been discussed. Many of which address this rule. However, the point here is to not

think that you can pretend to be one person with the intention of getting married, and then change to another. This is an easy way to get divorced. Secondly, make sure you confirm that he wants what you want in life. If he wants 4 kids now and wants to move to China before you get married, don't think you are going to change him and renegotiate what he wants to no children and living in Kentucky. It's better to do it before you get to the alter, than to wait for your opportunity to discuss these items in divorce court.

Rule #13:
Never allow yourself to be manipulated by GSF: Guilt, Shame or Fear.

Explanation:
Part of what controls our actions in making decisions is our guilt, shame and fear regarding past actions. When we use the knowledge to make us wiser in the future, that's wisdom. When we place these items in a dark closet, that's GSF.

Your wife left you; you got an abortion; you're an unwed mother. I'm sure at various points in time these items were all considered strictly taboo, but not anymore. Because they just don't happen to others anymore. They happen to the man down the street and the lady on your block. Through open forums the items in the closet are coming out, and when that happens, it's no longer GSF. Everyone knows and the power and control it once held over you starts to dwindle. All of a sudden, those important things just don't have the great hold anymore. The GSF is gone and all that remains are the lessens learned, which only make you wiser on the next go round in the Mating Game.

Rule #14:
What you put up with is what you will have.

Explanation:
Now I know that a relationship is filled with give and take. However, I've known too many women that were giving, while he was taking. Giving and taking in one direction is not the making of a good relationship. You can fool yourself into believing that what your relationship is, is not what it will be (in the future) and that it will get better. However, the bottom line of truth is that "what you put up with today, is what you will have tomorrow."

If you select a guy who is a user and is using you today, chances are he's going to be using you tomorrow. If you date a woman who likes to have several guys on-call and that's what you put up with today, chances are that's what you will put up with tomorrow. Too many people want to glorify the prospect of change and depend too heavily on the belief in a different tomorrow without a real commitment from the individual who is suppose to be doing the change. A boat load of empty promises to change only make you complacent and accepting of standing in the exact same place tomorrow as you stood today, with the promise of a step forward tomorrow. However, as we all know, "tomorrow" never comes, because it's always a day away.

Rule #15:
With every privilege comes a responsibility.

Explanation:
We take for granted all of the fabulous opportunities we are given out of the normal course of our existence. However with every privilege also comes a responsibility. Being a parent is a privilege; properly raising the children is the responsibility that comes with that privilege. Having sex is a privilege, protecting others and yourself from disease and premature pregnancy is the responsibility that comes with that privilege. Most problems arise when we jump to accept the privilege and forget that the responsibility must immediately come also. Both the privilege and the responsibility are connected as one item and come as a package deal.

Rule #16:
You always know the answers.

Explanation:
Despite what you may disbelieve, within all of us lie the answers to all of our problems. It's not a miracle, and it's not unbelievable. You know everything there is to know about you. You know why you did or didn't do everything that's happened to you in your life. You know why you hesitated to accept a choice and why you regretted ones that made you unhappy. When people chose to ask

others "Is this right?" "...or should I do that?" It's only because they've either not started listening to themselves or they've finally taken the time to hear what they've been saying to themselves all along, but are not confident enough to take the step. Many just fail to trust that voice, which is to be expected. After all, it has been so long since they have listened to themselves, and old habits are difficult to break. It's understandable. These are usually life choices and decisions that are the most important. You want to be sure; however, sometimes you have to just take a leap of faith and trust yourself.

<u>Rule #17</u>
Money and personality do for men what cosmetics and a new outfit can do for women.

Explanation:
It's true what they say about, "beauty being in the eye of the beholder". Some of us "be holding" money and it sure looks BEAUTIFUL to me!

All jokes aside: to women, a strong sense of self-confidence, a sexy attitude and a firm body can be very attractive. Still to others it's all about the personality or what they can get, that makes someone attractive.

Beauty is without a doubt, extremely subjective. What one person thinks is attractive is not what another thinks is attractive. However, there seems to be a consistent theme with regard to men with women that relates back to money. This is

because, just as discussed in the section of this book entitled, "Tools of the Trade" money can represent a variety of things. A man with money to a woman could mean that he has:
- direction in his life,
- a career path,
- confidence,
- a sense of security (both financial and emotional), or
- the ability to just plain buy you things!!

Any way you put it, whether it's an ugly man with money or an attractive man with money, to a woman men with money just plain LOOK better!

Rule #18:
Women are like stocks. They are unpredictable, and unless you have one that is highly rated, top grade and reliable, you are better off with more than one to diversify your risk of instability.

Explanation:
It's no secret that men like to have more than one woman in their life. Truth is that that's normally called dating. It's not suppose to be an illegal activity, but when each one of the many women think they are the only one in his life, then matters start to get sticky. Women don't expect men to have a diversified portfolio of women. Women don't expect it because it usually means that he's still playing around and women tend to move toward

wanting to settle down and generally expect men to do the same.

However, with all due respect, both men and women should be able to meet other people through the course of dating prior to mating or marriage. It's necessary to learn about ourselves, have fun as well as to find out more about what is important on an on-going basis. However, men use it to have a pair and a spare in case one goes crazy.

Rule #19:
A promise without conviction is an ultimatum without consequence or value.

Explanation:
How many times have you heard a parent yell out a child's name in a shopping mall or grocery store pleading with him not to continue with a certain activity only to have the child continue anyway? If you've been to as many stores as I have, the answer would be many times. Why do you suppose the child didn't pay any attention to the parent's threats? Obviously, because the parent's threats were only promises without conviction and the child knew that because the parent had constantly proven that he/she had no intention of providing the child with a consequence, there was no reason to stop.

If a child can learn that promises without consequence are not threats, why wouldn't an adult be able to realize the same thing? Answer: they would, and that is why, women that continue to threaten their cheating husbands or boyfriends with leaving (or leave only to come back again and again) doesn't work. Because like a child, the adult knows an empty promise when he sees one.

Rule #20:
Periodically FREAK! --Freeze for a Reality Examination, Accepting Knowledge.

Explanation:
In the course of living life, sometime we need time to get off the fast moving train to take a look at where the train is going. Sometimes where we thought we we're going is not where we were headed. Sometimes the train could have taken a turn, unannounced to you and sometimes what we think we see is not what's really there at all. So, in order to avoid being taken for a ride, the best think to do is every now and then, take a moment to stand back and just FREAK:
Freeze for a
Reality
Examination,
Accepting
Knowledge.

The new information could change your perspective or just make you appreciate the ride.

Rule #21:
The person least in love and least dependent can always win.

Explanation:

In the Mating Game, players in the beginning stages of development prior to the phase of Intimacy (explicitly: The Hunt, Discovery and Friendship) feel a greater since of freedom to walk away. Although everyone should feel that same freedom at every stage, individuals within this window of the relationship recognize that a long-term commitment has not yet been made. These individuals feel compelled to "speak now or forever hold their peace." In the process, it always appears that the individual least in love is also the person who is least dependent and able to break away.

This individual usually has all of the needed forms of sustaining themselves without NEED for the other. There being together is purely a matter of PREFERENCE. This person has financial security, emotional stability, existing companionship, family, etc. However, for the person most in love there strong desire to remain in the relationship (more often than not) appears to be a matter of pure NECESSITY.

This is probably why, stay-at-home wives are encouraged to have a secret savings of money all their own. Because they would otherwise be completely dependent on the relationship for their financial stability. It's probably also why a person who has a poor understanding of self is greatly encouraged to maintain his/her own separate life and identity (outside of the relationship) and an individual with a poor connection to his/her family is encouraged to attempt to mend their broken family ties (when possible). All in all, if neither person walks away, the growth prompted by this development would create two stronger individuals and two stronger people, eventually also make a stronger couple. And if they do breakup, they breakup as stronger people, which is how it should be. This way both people create a win-win regardless of what happens.

<u>**Rule #22:**</u>
For women, love is a life sentence. For men, love is a contract breakable by demand: married or not.

Explanation:
For women, marriage is " 'til death do us part". For men, marriage is " 'til someone better do we part" By now we should all know that all little girls do NOT grow-up to immediately marry the prince and live happily ever after. In fact, in reality, we all know how the real story of Cinderella ended. For all the world, Princess Diana was our Cinderella. So, we know that in the real version of Cinderella, right after the Prince and Cinderella drove off in the horse drawn carriage, the Prince immediately fathered two children with Cinderella, (in between his visits to his mistress) and then divorced

Cinderella, toke away her title, threatened to keep her children and as soon as she dies a short-lived life, he goes off into the sunset with his mistress and two sons to live happily ever after.

Marriage is obviously "NOT" guaranteed, nor is it forever. Marriage is instead a promise to try to commit. Therefore, after everyone has said their "I do," don't be surprised if "you don't".

Rule #23:
Predictability can be dangerous.

Explanation:
People who cheat do so based on predictability. Have you ever wondered how a person could be comfortable cheating in the very bed they share with their husband or wife? That comfort comes from the predictability of their mate:
- she always comes home after 5:00pm;
- he always goes bowling on Thursday Night;
- she always takes three hours to get her hair done.

This is predictability and the best way to get out of being predictable is to sporadically be unpredictable. Do the opposite of what you said you would do; change your plans in the middle: come home early, take an early lunch, get your nails done and skip the hair. Change things around a bit without notice and see what happens. You may find something interesting. You may be pleasantly surprised that everything is as it appears or you may be in for a rude wakeup call. Either way, it's all good.

Rule #24:
There will always be someone else to replace a lost member of the harem.

Explanation:
Regardless of the game you decide to play or not play, there will always be someone willing to replace you. I've heard several women say that they will not leave a questionable relationship, but instead choose to try to change a man. Their logic is "why should I give him up and let some other woman have him?" Answer: because he's playing by a different set of rules that don't include yours. Regardless of how raw or disgusting a player may be, there always seems to be some unsuspecting player ready to accept the terms of the Game. However, you can't worry about that and you can't worry about the fact that he or she will have someone else after you leave. Because the simple fact is that whether you leave now or later, there will always be somebody else willing to take your place in the harem and if you are going to leave, you're better off leaving now rather than later after you've given more of your precious time away.

Rule #25:
"Need" can easily be mistaken for "Love".

Explanation:
> When a person says, "I love you," what they really mean is "I need you". If you remove the world love and force yourself to explain what you mean, you will find that what you really mean to say is:
- I ENJOY the time we spend together.
- I APPRECIATE the way she treats me.
- I DEPEND on his financial stability.
- I NEED him to be around.
- I'm AFRAID of being alone.
- I NEED a sense of belonging.
- I'm AFRAID of not finding someone.

…and the list goes on and on. So, remove the word "love" and find out what you really mean.

Rule #26:
> ***Thou shall not share with others intimate details and family secrets.***

Explanation:
> This rule is without a doubt among the most sacred of the lot. Many women have created the most devious and powerful monsters of relationship destruction through simply breaking this rule and sharing the intimate details of her relationship. Women like to talk and tend to talk to all the wrong people. Her best girlfriend is the most likely culprit to take advantage of this insider information and be all that he wants her to be. Before you know what hit you, she's living in your house, with your man, doing all that she can to please him.

Rule #27:
Play your own game.

Explanation:
    If the winner of the game is bound to be the one who understands the rules the best, why not be the one who creates the rules? ...not that everyone in the world has to play by them, just the people that want to play with you.

Rule #28:
Illusions can be a player's best friend.

Explanation:
    Just as was previously mentioned, things aren't always as they seem. What you see is not necessarily what you get. A well-dressed man in a fancy car with a roll of bills is not necessarily a rich man with a car. A woman with a large breast line and long hair is not necessarily an attractive woman with big breasts and long hair. A player in the Mating Game who has decided to use deception to get what he or she wants will make you believe that what you see is what you get, just long enough for him/her to get what he/she wants. Recognizing that illusion is constantly being used is an important thing to be aware of before, during and after entering into a relationship.

The Bottom line...
    So, now that you know how everyone else is playing the game, take a moment and create your

The Rules

own rules to play by. And if people don't want to play by your rules, kick them to the curb. Once you've set your rules, don't make exceptions for players who try to change your rules. Accept no substitutions for the original rules! Because remember, if the rules are your rules, you will always win, regardless of whether you are with someone or not. However, watch out for the art of deception that some call "LYING!"

Chapter 6

The Art of Lying

■ ■ ■

Creating the Magic of Illusion through Words

To those of us who have ever experienced a lie in it's truest form, you know that lying is an art. To create an illusion with words, makes the world a better place in the end, for the person who is being lied to. With one swoop of the spoken word a master of deception can erase uncertainty and make the world seem just a little brighter. And with just a few more well placed words, doubt turns into a passing thought and anger blossoms into an apology. It's the art of illusion and is no less a form of magic than the disappearing assistant: now you see the doubt and concern, add a lie and now you DON'T! Lying is a form of communication and just like magic, it is an art, the art of deception.

"It's the embedded lie that you want to avoid," added a 28-year old Fun Phil from DC whom I like to call "Tony-Tone'-Toni" (after the singing group). The embedded is a lie, within a lie, within a lie that keeps going until you can't lie about the lie anymore because you start to forget the lies you told. There are too many to remember and the lies start to contradict each other. There are a variety of lying methods that can convince a woman to put back on her rose colored glasses (or blinders) and be manipulated by the control statements. The most common way of lying is patching.

Patching is simple enough. Some women call it "Tell Me What I Want To Hear". And simply put, it's just that. You tell him where the problems are with his story and he creates a new story for each problem area that you have kindly informed him of. In essence, he is not creating an entirely new lie; instead he is Patching his old existing ones. But while this is the simplest form, it can also easily lead to the embedded lie, if you are not careful. Typically, patching is only successful if you need to use it once or twice. Beyond that, it can be dangerous and put you in a complicated tangled web. If you intend to lie on a more frequent basis, you should lean toward coupling patching with one of the other methods discussed within this chapter or select another method all together, like as...

The Classical Method: Get Mad First!

This method has been around forever: because it works. If you are in a discussion and you're losing, then immediately become offensive and take the stance first. It is important that you jump to the offensive mode *first*, because then you stop answering questions and become the one asking the questions. You are immediately placed in control.

Now that you are in the driver's seat, the other person is left busy trying to answer your questions and satisfy your questions. So much so, that they will either forget the question that they were initially asking of you or will table the discussion for another time for fear of making you any angrier.

Why does this method work? Because the person who is being confronted with this method is actually being confronted with the fear of losing the other person. That's why the individual that uses this method, must provide an important element to the person he or she is using this method on that she is afraid of losing. That thing does not have to be love and most times it isn't.

Think about it. You are the girlfriend. Your boyfriend accuses you of being with another man. If you are not a good liar or don't want to be bothered with remembering inconsistencies in your lies then "The Getting Mad First" Method is an easy and quick method to use. Because as soon as you jump to use this method, you don't have to answer any more questions. It works a little something like this:

Shana walks in the door at 1:00am and is met by her live-in boyfriend, Todd.

"So, where were you?" Todd asks.

"You know I went out with my girls." Shana responds.

"Well, if that's true, then why did Wanda tell me that you were on your way home 2 hours ago?"

"Wait a minute. Are you questioning me? Because I know you are not questioning me!"

"Well, what do you expect for me to do?" Todd interjects.

"No! I am not even going to get into this. I cannot believe you don't trust me! I mean, have I ever given you a reason not to trust me? And what is a relationship without trust? Are you trying to tell me that we don't have trust? Because I can't live with someone who doesn't trust me. Hell, I can't even go out with my girlfriends without getting the third degree when I get home! What the Hell is up with that!"

"Well, Shana..." Todd begins

She interjects "NO!! Don't say another word! I don't want to hear it!" Shana calms down for a moment and then says, "I'm going to bed."

Do you see how well that works? You take it to the offensive level before he does. If he is not willing to go there, then he will back up out of fear of things getting out of hand. Even if he does take it to the next level, it doesn't matter. You don't have to answer anything, you have not told any lies to remember and both you and he can walk away at the same level of anger. That means that you do not necessarily have to initiate the apology to him later. You both can apologize to each other and neither one losses face. Or you can appear to be the bigger person by apologizing first for getting mad and make out like a bandit. However, you are not apologizing for your actions. That would be to admit guilt or wrong doing and that could hurt you next time. You admit to getting angry and can apologize for that. You can even apologize for not calling, because next time when you stay out late, it just means you have to make a phone call, and it's all good.

The Convenient Memory and Hearing Loss Method

What do you do when you tried to lie your way out of a mess and have now told so many lies that you can't remember what they were or your guy has found some inconsistencies in your stories and you are about to go down for the count? Use this method: the Convenient Memory and Hearing Loss Method.

What is it? This is a way of cleaning up the inconsistencies with the excuse that someone didn't hear what was said correctly or by questioning someone's memory recalling the facts. It is not a difficult method, but it is extremely useful. Think about it. How many times do people bring their own memory or what they heard into question? Well, you are now using that known flaw against them.

The beauty of this method is that people will tell you exactly where the inconsistency lies and you only have to correct the problem area. Now, true enough, you are using a form of "patching", but what allows you this freedom is your ability to question the facts using memory and hearing as an excuse.

You have to listen to what is being said and how it is being said, because the person is going to tell you exactly what he does or doesn't want you to say. Listen carefully and he will tell you the correct answers that he/she wants you to give. For example, she will say, "I know you didn't go to Rachel's house?" She has just told you that the correct answer is NOT to be at Rachel's house. So, you respond with, "Of course, I was not at Rachel's house! Why the Hell would I be at Rachel's house?" Now, in reality, where were you really? You were at Rachel's house. Now, this is how a conversation might go. Let's use the same two people, Todd and Shana in the same situation now using this method:

Shana comes in again at 1:00am only to meet Todd her live in boyfriend.

Todd begins, "Shana, it's 1:00am where have you been?"

"You know I was out with my girls," Shana answers.

"Well, why is it that one of your girls told me that you would be home 2 hours ago?"

Shana responds, "What?"

Todd continues, "Your girl said you were on your way home 2 hours ago."

Shana responds, "That girl, I don't know what her problem is. I told her I was going to hang around for another hour or two, but it was so loud in that club, she probably couldn't hear me."

Todd continues, "Well, whatever, the least you could have done was call."

"Todd, I told you yesterday, that me and my girls were going to stay out late. So, I don't understand why you are getting so upset about this. I told you we were going out and even mentioned that I really didn't expect to be back before midnight."

"I don't remember you saying that?" Todd responds.

"Well, I did. If I hadn't already told you that I was going to be out later than normal in advance, I would understand your reaction now, but I had my girls call you, just to make sure you knew. But it was just a simple mistake. It's not my fault girlfriend couldn't hear me. It was loud in that club. But, Todd, come on now. You must remember me telling you. I knew I was going to be out later because there were several things happening at the club tonight. That was the reason we wanted to go in the first place. Remember?"

"Well, I guess if you already told me, but I just don't remember that." Todd says.

"You must have been half listening, because we were sitting down talking when I told you. In fact, I think you were watching that football game you were talking about "

Do you see how it works?. Most guys don't really listen to everything anyway. Did you see how she threw that football item in at the end? He was still having doubts and needed some additional assurance, so she told him that it happened during the football game. You can, of course, substitute any sport that your guy is passionate about in place of football. Everybody knows that many things can be said during a sporting event and not be heard by a man to save a life. Hell, most guys know they try to tune women out during the time they're watching their favorite sporting events anyway. So, it all works out!

The Silent Soldier Method: Say Nothing

Fear is a very useful tool in lying. If a person fears losing something that you bring to the relationship, that fear of loss and loneliness is greater than the pain of accepting infidelity or worse. If there is a fear of being incomplete without that person, you don't have to say anything. Why? Because the person will talk themselves into staying. I don't care how adamant or passionate you think she is or how self-confident and attractive you believe her to be. Fear is a monster that is not partial to anyone. It is an equal opportunity inhibitor, and can make the most confident person question his or herself.

Everyone experiences fear. It's how you deal with it that makes the difference. Well, with the

Silent Soldier Method, you don't have to say a word, nor do you have to lie? Because fear will make the other person lie to him or herself. It's a form of denial due to the fear of being alone or some other sense of loss on a greater scale. The conversation would go something like this, again using the same two people in the same situation:

Again, Shana walks in at 1:00am. Todd approaches her.

"Shana, where were you? Your girl said that you were going to be home hours ago!"

Shana looks at him with disbelief that he is asking the question.

He continues, "That is so inconsiderate! I can't believe you did this, Shana! What am I suppose to do sitting here worrying about you? The least you could have done is call. Don't you have anything to say for yourself?"

Shana says nothing.

"I didn't think so! And do you know why? Because, there is no excuse! You stay out all night, not a word. What were you thinking?

Shana says nothing and walks toward the bedroom.

Todd responds as he follows, "You weren't thinking! ...not of anybody except yourself."

Shana selects a night gown and goes into the bathroom to take a shower. Todd follows.

"You know how late it is?" Todd screams to be heard over the water from the shower as Shana showers. "It's late, Shana! Hell, I should be in bed now, but I was waiting up for you. You could have called."

Shana continues to shower, still not saying a word.

"Did you try to call? I guess you could have tried to call. But I didn't get any call; if you did, you should have tried a little harder!"

Shana turns off the shower, gets out dries off, puts on her gown and walks into the bedroom; Todd follows.

"I still don't understand why you couldn't call." Todd looks Shana straight in the eyes. Shana looks at him with disbelief again and gets into bed and closes her eyes.

Todd finishes, "Well, we will talk about this in the morning. Oh, hell, I'm going to sleep."

True, this method is not for everyone. You have to take a lot of yelling sometimes and not everyone can keep their cool. Why does this method work? Because it takes two to fight. One person can't fight for long by his or herself. After a while of talking to yourself, rationalization kicks in and you start looking for your own answers. Also, you get tired and just give up.

Tell Me What I Want To Hear

People are funny creatures. They will tell you exactly what they want to hear, as we previously discussed. This is of course "patching" taken to the next level. Just follow this example:

"Shana, where were you? You obviously weren't at the club. Your girl said you would be home hours ago."

Now obviously, he has already told you that to tell him that you were at the club will not be an acceptable answer. This is were we use a thing called a "pill". A pill is a lie coated with a slight truth. These pills are easy to swallow and go down so smoothly. Watch and learn.

Shana responds, "You're right. I was not at the club. I left when the girls left".

"I knew you did." he responds. "So, where were you?"

Now, the truth is you met some guy and went to his place and had a little sexual chocolate, but that's not the answer we can give.

"I left the club but didn't feel like going home, so I went to a couple of bars and had a few drinks. Saw some friends and lost track of time." ...which is all true; you just excluded a few important items.

Sounds good doesn't it? But it's only a small piece of the truth. See, he knows you were not at the club; he has already told you that you were not there. If you admit to that piece of known information, you can lie about the rest and he will think that because you confessed to one piece of information, you are now being 100% honest, when in fact, you are only being 10% honest. That is what we call a "pill".

The Method of Complete Disbelief: Me or Your Lying Eyes

Now this is a method that should not be used unless you are confident of the control you have over your subject. Eddie Murphy talked about it in one of his comedy movies. You may remember:

A man is caught butt naked in bed with another women. He is actively having sex with her. Both of them are sweaty from hot steamy sex. The man turns to see his wife standing in the doorway.

He stands up and is naked with an erection and he says to his wife, "Now, baby, this is not what you think. It's not what it looks like."

She says, "It is exactly what it looks like! I can't believe you did this to me!" She begins crying and losing control. He follows, still naked with an erection.

His wife yells out with tears in her eyes, "You fucked her!!".

He then replies, "Yes, I fucked her! I fucked her! Is that what you think? Then yes, you are right, I fucked her!" He pauses for a moment and then continues. "I fucked her. ...but I make love to you."

That is what I call "Me or Your Lying Eyes" All the evidence is there, but again fear is a great inhibitor and can stop you from having true happiness. Her fear of being alone, her fear of losing the game, made her accept a shitty excuse like that. Why? Because he knew that she was looking for a way to rationalize what he had done. So, he gave it to her, and if she is desperate enough, she will accept his excuse. Because it's more painful to believe that he loves someone else, than to believe he still loves his wife and just had sex with someone else. However, just because I used Eddie Murphy's example doesn't mean that women don't do this too, because they do.

The Last Chance
...to Dance Methods

When you're lying, you are generally dancing around the truth. And even though several of the methods can be used together and are very effective either way, sometimes people refuse to fall for them. When would this happen? When reality is starting to set in or the fear of your cheating boyfriend leaving is becoming less important in your life, or would be less painful. These are some tid bits to use in those instances.

The "That's Not Fair" Method:
"Appeal to the person's sense of fairness."

There will be times when your guy will make a statement that is completely valid that you have absolutely no response for.

Like what? Well, like how you were not there one night for an important business dinner that he asked you to attend weeks in advance. So, how do you respond to that? You simply say, "That's not fair." You appeal to his sense of fairness and attempt to have him eliminate the item completely from the discussion by giving him the excuse you gave before and then remind him that that was an accident, not purposeful; therefore, it doesn't count.

A Taste of the Truth
If your guy has gotten to the point that he is tired of your lies and is no longer accepting your

excuses, and he is firmly taking a stance not to accept another lie. Then this is a matter of damage control. If he is telling you what happened and is so confident that you did it that he is going to believe you did it whether you say you did or didn't. Then, you have to resort to final measures. Admit that what he says is true.

Why would you do that? Remember this is damage control. You have been lying to him all along the way. If you have reached this point, he is probably thinking about or on the verge of leaving you. If you want him to stay for whatever reason, then you admit to what he says you did, because remember you've done much worse. You are just admitting to a small fraction of what you have really done. However, if it has gotten to this point, you have not been giving him enough truth to hold on to in your "pills". So now you have to overcompensate by giving him a large dose of the truth. Don't admit to anything more than he is telling you, unless it is necessary. You will be able to tell from the conversation. Remember, people will tell you what they want to hear.

Why would you do this? Because, if you give him that little ounce of satisfaction in knowing that he is right, in his mind, you have now opened up and been honest with him, period. You have now cleared the way for a new batch of deception. Just make sure that you mix your pills properly with the right amount of lie and truth, this time.

Reading Between the Lies

Carol was a very sweet young woman who had a boyfriend, Alvin. Alvin and Carol had agreed to get married in two years, right after Alvin finished getting his second degree. He worked long hours and so did Carol. However, Alvin worked during the day and went to school at night. She knew how difficult that could be, so she made every attempt to give Alvin all the time and space he needed. She didn't call him as much and she didn't demand that much of his time as a person in an intimate game (relationship) might. Instead, she let Alvin come to her when he had time. That was her way of helping him. However, in the process, Carol didn't really have a partner to go out with, so she decided to put her energies into her job, working longer hours. "Might as well do something constructive with the time," she thought.

Well, Alvin had just started his final year and Carol thought that maybe they could spend more time together then. So, one day when Carol went over to Alvin's apartment to surprise him with an evening picnic: a reward for his hard work. She saw Alvin coming out of the main doors of his apartment building with another female.

At first Carol was shocked, then she thought maybe they are just studying. That is what she allowed herself to think for 3 seconds before Alvin leaned toward this woman and kissed her in a way that Carol had not been kissed in a long while.

Obviously, Carol was stunned. She sat in her car for 180 seconds, counting each one, until her mind caught up with her body. Her thoughts were racing forward. Carol was not the confrontational type, so she had to calm down and think. So, she decided to drive home, it was getting late.

When she arrived at her apartment, she was still thinking about what she had seen. She couldn't think about anything else. Sitting by the phone, she finally decided to make that call. She dialed Alvin's number and a woman's voice answered; Carol hung up. Now, she was even more confused. Was there more than one? Did the woman she saw come back? Are they having a study session with several women in the group? Again questions were racing and still no answers. Then, she thought, maybe that was the wrong number. So, she dialed the number again, and this time Alvin answers the phone.

"Alvin?"

"Yes, who is this?" he replied

"This is Carol."

"Hi, what's new?"

"Alvin, did a woman just pick up your phone?"

"Well, yes, I have a friend here that I'm trying to help out with a few things."

"Oh...well, I just left your apartment and saw you with some woman?"

"Woman, that couldn't have been me, I've been up here taking care of this project."

"Alvin, I know what you look like and it was you. Not only that, but you kissed her, lips to lips, Alvin. What is going on here!"

"That must of been a brief moment when I went down stairs to make sure she got in her car okay."

"But, Alvin, you kissed her, with feeling. I saw that Alvin. You kissed her!"

"Carol, you are seeing things. Yes, I kissed her but not lips to lips. I swear to you. She is having a rough time right now, so, I was trying to let her know that she was not alone."

All of a sudden, Carol hears a third voice, enter the conversation on a third phone, "Who needs encouragement?" the third voice responded.

Carol responded, "He said you needed some encouragement, that's why he kissed you."

All of a sudden he said, "Let me call you back."

Carol felt a rush in her body, and then she asked herself, "What the Hell just happened?" That's when she called me, and told me the entire story. I immediately said to her, "Girl, he's mending the damaged bridges right now!"

"What?" Carol replied.

"He is mending the damage that your call just created. Right now; he is talking to this other girl, lying in order to undo what you just did. You need to call him back and talk to her."

Of course, this was a surprise for Carol. She wanted to believe what Alvin said so much that she closed her eyes to the reality of the matter and allowed herself to be lied to. It was so uncharacteristic of her to take a confrontational role and Alvin knew that. And I knew that he was counting on that.

Carol went on to say that at some point during the conversation she had just had with Alvin, that Alvin had offered to let her talk to the other woman. And I knew that the only reason that Alvin did so was because he knew how Carol's mind worked. Carol believed in trust in a relationship. To speak to this other person, would have implied that she couldn't trust him and trust was what she felt every relationship was based on. So, Carol would not demand to talk to anybody; she was very predictable. And that was in part, her problem.

So, even though it was now close to midnight, Carol did as I had instructed, on pure faith, (the unpredictable) and called Alvin back. Alvin answered the phone.

"Let me talk to her." Carol said.

"Talk to who?" Alvin replied.

And at the top of her lungs she replied, "I said let me TALK TO HER DAMN IT!!"

Another woman's voice picked up the phone and then their were three.

And with the politest voice from Carol she said, "Hi, I'm Carol and your name is...?"

And with a voice that was both smooth and calm, the voice replied, "Julie."

Carol responded, "That's a nice name. So are you sleeping with Alvin?"

Alvin then interjected, "I DON'T BELIEVE WE ARE TALKING ABOUT THIS!"

See, you can lie to one when the other is not on the line. But how do you continue the lies to both when you have to respond with one answer to accommodate both people. How do you keep both lies going to both women, when they are both listening?

Julie responded, "Yes, I am."

"How long have you been sleeping with Alvin, Julie?"

Alvin then again interjected, "I CAN'T BELIEVE YOU ARE TALKING ABOUT MY BUSINESS!"

Carol then raised her tone slightly in response to that stupid statement and said:

"WE are your business." to say that his business included and affected them and was not just about HIM. Therefore, they had every right to discuss it. Carol went back to her calm tone and Julie answered the question.

"For six months, I have been sleeping with Alvin. I moved in here almost immediately after we met. Alvin asked me to."

Carol was shocked, not just about Julie being a resident in Alvin's apartment, not just about how she had not recognized the problem for 6 months, but that Alvin is the one that brought her into this relationship. Julie said that Alvin pursued her. All this time, Carol was sitting at work giving him time to study. Well, this was definitely not the kind of study that Carol thought he was doing. And all the nights when Carol didn't call thinking that he needed time, she didn't think it was for THIS. Within an instant, her illusion of Alvin was shattered. He was not the person she thought he was. He was now a liar, a cheat, a conspiring bastard. Within that moment, a single instant, Carol felt that she, for the first time, knew who Alvin was. It was like having someone you care about die, only to be introduced to his evil twin who to your surprise you've been dating for a few years now. Carol then added.

"Do you do any wild sexual stuff?"

Alvin then jumped in, "What!"

Julie replied, "No."

The answer then shattered another myth that Carol had. When Carol and Alvin were together, Alvin had been asking her to do some wild sexual positions that Carol didn't want to do. When she was asking Julie these questions, the thought came to mind that wild sex might be why he was with Julie. Carol thought that maybe Alvin strayed because she wouldn't cave into a simple sexual request he made one night. Maybe the reason Julie was with Alvin was because she didn't give into doing these sexual positions, but Julie just answered that question. The answer was no. Alvin couldn't understand how calm both Carol and Julie were in talking about this entire thing. I suppose he thought that from his perspective he was still going to be able to have his cake and eat it too. So, in the wake of his comfort and within the moment of silence, he said:

"You two are talking to each other as though you are old girlfriends." Carol could hear him smile on the phone.

Carol then responded with the same calm demeanor: "She hasn't done anything to me. YOU HAVE! She didn't know anything about me. You DID. YOU brought her into this relationship! She didn't owe me anything. You did. YOU have done this to me." And with that Carol slammed the phone down.

The next day, Alvin called Carol at work. "For what?" you might ask. Amazingly enough, to try to get his cake back, so he could eat it too. Yep, he tried to lie to Carol to cover up that Julie was still living at his house. Simply amazing. Carol wouldn't take the calls at first. Then she started to feel weak. You see, unknown to Carol, she wore some Pretty Colored Chains. Carol was a Golden Girl. And while Carol didn't initially know that, Alvin did. He knew what his role was in Carol's life and he knew he could use it. So, in the end, despite it all, Carol did consider trying to win Alvin back. But that would have been playing right into Alvin's hands. He wanted her to try to win him back in a Coochie Competition!

In a Coochie Competition between two battling women, He could get any kind of sex he wants. He would become the man of the evening. To be the focus of a Coochie Competition is a position of privilege. To be fought over by two women, each trying to out do the other constantly, for a man, is a position rivaled only by heaven. What woman or man would not want to be the object of desire with absolute card-blanche to sex any kind, anywhere at any time?

Thank goodness, Carol thought the whole thing through, before she did anything. She called him up one day, again because she was feeling weak and told him to chose one of us. That was it, chose one woman.

She gave him a couple of days and called him for his decision, and again he used his finely tuned ability to lie to make it seem as though he could not just throw Julie out because she had no where to go. However, during their midnight conversation among the three of them, Julie had also confessed to Carol that she had family in town and she had a job, so Julie's decision to live at Alvin's was not a matter of her not having another place to stay. Julie's decision to stay there was by choice, just as Alvin's desire to have her there was by choice. So, in that instance of Alvin attempting to weasel out of the situation, Carol finally opened her eyes and saw the situation for what it was and said:

"You've already made your decision. You simply failed to tell me about it." and with that she hung up the phone. After that, Carol started to think things through clearly and started to work out ways to replace the Pretty Colored Chains she wore that were attached to Alvin. Carol discovered that she was fun dependent on Alvin. So she started doing really nice things for herself. It was the beginning of a wonderful life.

Alvin actually had the audacity to call Carol back numerous times again! He left several messages on her voice mail, but Carol refused to return the call. As time passed and with effort made, Carol was well on her way to being a stronger person. She was happy, and as luck would have it, she accidentally picked up the phone one day when she was in a hurry on the way out. Yes, it was Alvin.

"Julie is moving out"

"Why don't you just save your money"

"It's over between Julie and me." Then he gave that said hurt puppy dog act that she could hear through the phone that was suppose to make a any Dr. Cindy want to jump through the phone and comfort him.

Then the reality of the entire situation that he had put her through slapped Carol in the face. He had lied to her, led her to believe that he was too busy for her, manipulated her into being okay with half of the type of relationship that she wanted while she thought he was studying and cheated on her for 6 months, while she provided him with the time to do it! And she snapped and replied, "HEY!! Stop lying to me!" But Alvin continued lying, so Carol interjected again, " HEY!! Don't Play ME!! Play the Lottery! You've got a better chance of winning!!" And with that she hung up the phone.

From that entire ordeal, not only did Carol discover that it was not something she had done, but that it was not about her. That goes along way. Can you imagine the thoughts that she might have crippled herself with, had she not spoken to Julie during that three person conference call? Can you imagine the life Carol would have had being married to someone that she would have only later discovered never really knew had she named Alvin? That is a scary thought. The other woman, did Carol a favor. Not only did she allow Carol the opportunity to walk away with answers, but she indirectly gave Carol an opportunity to look to herself and make some changes that would positively affect her for a lifetime. Sometimes a breakup is a blessing in disguise

How to Avoid the Lies

Despite how unbelievable it may seem, some people don't appreciate being lied to. However, people that constantly accept a lie, do so because they feel they need it or would prefer it over the truth. Some lies are so obvious, while others are a little more challenging to spot. However, if you want to know how to spot and detect a lie, the following would be how you would do it.

1. Listen With Your Eyes. A person can say anything, but it's what they do that's important. A man can say he loves you, but if he is loving everybody else, does he? No. A man can say that he will always be there for you, but if he never comes home, is he? No. A man can tell you that he thinks you are beautiful, but if he is constantly criticizing how you look, does he? No. A man can tell you that you're the only one that he loves, but if you've already caught him loving three other women (and God knows how many more), does he really love only you? No.

2. Take It Like A Man. While I hate to admit it, women do get more emotional about relationship problems than men. In fact, women tend to act more on emotion than on fact and that is what I intend to address by the phrase, "Take It Like A Man".

When you are filled with emotion, you can't think clearly. This is one reason why people say, "sleep on it" or "let's talk about it tomorrow". It's because your judgment can be clouded by the present anger or sadness of the moment.

The more pain you experience, the more your mind tends to look for an easy way out (an escape route). Usually that exit is provided in the form of a lie (given by the person who has hurt you). That is why lies are so effective in painful situations. The brain does not want to accept the fact that it has been given inconsistencies or lies. When it is detected, the brain can exercise one of two options.

1. The first option is to realize the painful situation that you are in, and take the action needed to correct it.

2. The second option is to hold onto some false notion, promise or belief that things will get better, and continue on your same path.

Again, this is why lies are so effective and why you constantly hear that phrase, "I'm going to give him/her ONE more chance."

The brain knows that if something is wrong, something must change. The brain will constantly throw thoughts at you, if you do not correct the inconsistency in facts, and you will periodically encounter thoughts like:

- "How can you BE all that, if you put up with this crap?"

- "If any man would love to have you, why is your man loving everybody else?"

- "How can you be in control (period), if you don't even have control of this?"

Finally, you hit the thought, "This must not continue like it is!" When this final thought passes, the person in crisis voices an opinion and the wrong-doer says, "I will never do it again". At that point, you have the option of believing or just plain leaving.

Leaving, unfortunately, offers more hardships (emotional, financial, etc.) for the brain to contemplate processing. Believing in a new lie, offers immediate satisfaction that things will change and is absent the prospect of additional immediate pain through the hardship of leaving the relationship. This is why a person not in the situation can so easily see what needs to be done, because they can evaluate the situation without the threat of experiencing personal hardship or pain, but the person in the relationship cannot do this. There action is directly connected to their own pain or discomfort.

This is one of the reasons why a person should not get into a relationship to "supplement" things (emotional support, monetary stability, etc.) they need. A person that does so is only allowing to place themselves in a need dependent situation. The less a person uses a relationship to supplement his or her life, the greater the freedom they possess to enjoy a good relationship or to leave a bad one. In other words, stop believing (he will change) and start (forcing your change by) leaving.

3. *Do the Unexpected.* One of the key problems with women who are involved with players (be it Player Pete, Wham Bam Thank You Sam, Dollar

Bill, etc.) is that these players can play because they know these women better than they know themselves. He knows what she is going to do, when she is going to do it and how often each month she will get around to doing it. It is in many respects an extreme disadvantage to the woman.

One of the best ways to find out if your guy is lying or not (as mentioned in the chapter on the Art of Lying) is to every now and then, do the unexpected. Think about it. If he knows that you will never go to a club that he frequents, he will more than likely invite you down. So, do the unexpected and take him up on his offer; go to the club and see what's going on.

If he knows that every night you come home from work at 6:00pm, then come home from work early one day and see what's going on.

Whenever you do the unexpected, you can catch a man in a lie or verify that he's on the up and up. Either way, you're going to find out the truth.

4. *Don't Ignore Intuition.* Intuition is key. However, the very tool that can work for you can also work against you.

I was talking to a few guys the other day and Brian (a 29-year old friend from Florida) told me that around 8pm one evening a while back he had a feeling that something wasn't right. He didn't know what it was, but it was just a feeling that something bad was about to happen. At the time he was living with a roommate and ironically enough, that roommate came down and asked him if something didn't seem right. They both said that they had a feeling that something bad was about to happen. The entire situation was somewhat odd, given that everything seemed fine up until that point.

Both of the guys had female guests over. Their evenings had gone well, so both ended up in bed with their respective women, and both women were still in bed sleeping, when the guys got up to come to this unanimous conclusion.

So, Brian, got dressed and went outside to try to figure out why something didn't seem right. As he left his apartment, he saw his "first-tier girlfriend" drive up.

A "first-tier girlfriend" is a girlfriend given preferred treatment. It's similar to stock; preferred stock versus common, in that a "first-tier girlfriend" is preferred and a "second-tier girlfriend" is just plain common.

Anyway, after Brian ran outside to look around, he saw his first-tier girlfriend pull up into the parking lot of the apartment complex. So, he got in his car and drove away. Now, this wouldn't have been a big issue, I suppose, if she didn't have the key to his apartment, but she did. So, first-tier girlfriend goes up to his apartment, lets herself in and goes immediately to Brian's bedroom where to her surprise, she finds this other woman sleeping in her boyfriend's bed. Now, you might expect them to have "duked it out" (fought), but they didn't. Instead, they "had words" (talked). Unfortunately, it wasn't very productive, not because they were hateful. Compared to what they could have done, they were extremely calm. However, it was still unproductive, because the discussion didn't mean anything; it led to no new understanding of who should be there, nor any common ground about who maintained any current role (i.e.: present girlfriend). No one listened, both just spoke trying to convey their own point while not listening to a single word being said by anyone.

First-tier girlfriend told the woman in bed, "You know he does this all the time. You are just his female squeeze for tonight." Second-tier, just ignored her, put on her clothes and left.

Now, you may be thinking, "He is going to be in TROUBLE!" Well, if you WERE NOT thinking that, you were correct. He wasn't. When Brian saw his girlfriend's car drive into the parking lot, he drove away to a nearby gas station and called first-tier girlfriend's home number, leaving several messages that he was trying to reach her. When he finally spoke to her a day later, he just lied and said, "That woman always comes over and gets into my bed, when I'm not around". Obviously, she wanted to believe him. It was less painful to believe the lie, than to accept the entire reality of the truth, and so she did. First-tier girlfriend didn't "Take It Like A

Man". Brian obviously, used his own intuition recognizing that "Intuition Is Key" and listened to a funny feeling that he could not explain. It helped to get him out of a difficult situation and left his girlfriend in one.

Everybody knows that women have intuition, women just ignore it constantly. I have found that my intuition has been right not just in dealing with relationships, but in dealing with life. However, not many people acknowledge that men have the ability to feel and act on intuition too, because they do. So remember that the next time you decide to ignore your own. You could find yourself in a dangerous place.

Chapter

7

The Danger Zone

■ ■ ■

While we all like to think of the Mating Game as one big FUN adventure. The reality is that people can end up getting hurt all the time. We've all been there before. We may not have known were we were; some may have referred to it as a bad place, depression, or the pain of a breakup. However, despite what we may have called it, we all have been there or near the area at one point or another. This is the place I refer to as the Danger Zone. It's the place where you begin to question yourself, the place where you feel you keep accepting less. It's the place right before, during and after you get hurt from being in a relationship or by playing the Mating Game. And it's most definitely the place where you seem to begin to question your logic and reasoning.

The List!

Last year I went to New York to tape a talk show. This episode was called, "His Ex Thinks She's Hot, But She's Not!" All the women who called in were mad because their ex-boyfriends preferred their new girlfriends over them.

That's natural, right?

Well, there was disbelief, hurt, pain and anxiety because the ex-girlfriends all felt that they were better than their boyfriends' new girlfriends: better looking, better equipped, better mates, just an overall better match.

So, what was up with that? I'll tell you what it was. It was all about.. "The List". Think about it for a moment. Everything that you are and believe, is based on your experiences and the lessons you've learned from those experiences. So, let's pretend for a minute and go back to high school; which would be the first time most of us started really getting into the Mating Game. What was usually the thing that a guy would say to a female to let her know that he was interested in her? It was something like, "You are so pretty." Right? Right, and as time has moved on, that perception has NOT. The situation hasn't changed at all, except now the wording is: "You're so hot!" But the meaning remains.

With each go at the Mating Game, a woman is constantly told how attractive she is. Therefore, she begins to believe that she is beautiful and that being BEAUTIFUL is what got her the guy. Her physical beauty was the determining factor in attracting a guy. Am I right or am I right? I KNOW I'm right! And that is why these women thought that they should win these guys back in the Mating Game. The ex-girlfriends felt they were prettier, but what they were really referring to was "The List"!

"The List"? It's a combination of characteristics that we have developed over the years and carry in our heads that we refer and believe to be the MOST important characteristics, qualities or abilities to win the Mating Game every time. And of course at the top of a woman's list, for these ex-girlfriend's was:

1. the Finest!

They felt they had to be "the Finest, the Hottest or the Most Attractive" to win the Mating Game every time and believed that they were compared to these new women.

You see, if you've constantly been told by your boyfriends that he wanted to be with you because you were so attractive, you tend to believe that that is the most important item on your List. So, with each relationship that number one item becomes validated and your belief becomes firm that the most attractive woman wins the man. So you accept this belief.

With time, however, the bad acne goes away and women learn how to control their eating habits. So, what was a simple equation of "I am the finest" gets more difficult, because suddenly everyone is rather attractive. So, what's the determining factor now? Some women defer to the belief that, "I can sexually satisfy my man better than any other woman," the Queen Bee mentality. For the Queen Bee, that becomes their new number ONE item on the all mighty "List". However, complications set in when perception takes it's place to completely throw off any firm understanding that you might have once thought you had.

What am I talking about? Well, let's say looking fine is still at the top of your "List". Well, what's fine to you is not necessarily fine to him. In fact, we took five guys and showed them pictures of five women all dressed very differently:

- one woman in a tight revealing dress,
- one woman in an evening gown,
- one woman in a business suit,
- one woman in jeans and a T-shirt and,

- one woman in a casual summer dress.

Which woman do you think these five guys picked as the most attractive? I know most of you are thinking the woman in the tight dress, but of course, if the answer was that simple, I wouldn't have asked the question. So, guess again.

The answer is "no one particular woman"; that's the answer. When we gave these pictures to these men, they made their selections based on their OWN mental "Lists" which were based on their own set of experiences.

The first man had been burned in several relationships by women similar to the woman in the tight dress; so, he didn't think that woman was attractive at all. He thought she looked trashy and cold-hearted, but that was based on HIS personal experiences and HIS "List".

The second man said that he liked the woman that was dressed in the jeans and T-shirt because he was an out-doors kind of guy and liked women that didn't mind getting dirty, going hiking and doing sporty stuff.

The third guy said that he liked glamorous women. So, we naturally thought he was going to pick the woman in the evening gown. But then he said, "but I really don't like brunettes, I prefer red heads; they're more fun. So, I'll have to go with the lady in the casual dress".

The fourth guy said that he liked a woman that liked to do anything to please her man. Therefore, we thought he was going to say he liked the woman in the tight dress, because she was the most seductive, but he said: "So, I'm going to have to go with the woman in the business suit." We asked him why. He said that women in suits were the biggest freaks he had ever met.

The fifth guy looked at all of the pictures and said he thought they were all attractive, but he liked short women; so, he picked the shortest woman in the group. Why, I don't know because he was seven feet tall. (I know what you're thinking, but I'm not going there.)

So, back to our original story. How did these women on the show get there? They had formed their own "Lists" and just as we had said, with each relationship they believed more and more that being the "finest" and being the best "sexually" were the determining factors to winning a guy's heart. However, this time it didn't work and it was difficult for them that another woman, who was in their eyes less attractive, took away their men.

From the choices these men made on the show, you could tell that there were other things that were important to them for them to have chosen these other women. In some of the women, we could see their zest for life, a pleasant disposition, a care-free attitude, a determination, dedication or persistence in something other than pursuing him.

While the fact that it takes more than a pretty face and a sexually active body to win each round at the Mating Game may be obvious to us (if for no other reason than our brief five-man survey results previously discussed), it was not obvious to them. We tend to forget that he has a say in the type of person he wants too. It's not solely our decision. HIS perception is 50% of the equation (decision).

"Being physically attractive" may be an item of importance to both of you, but what he perceived as attractive, may not be what YOU see as attractive.

On this show, one of the new girlfriends weighed close to 250 pounds. The ex-girlfriend probably weighed in at 160, while the boyfriend was a slender, tall 170. So, for the ex-girlfriend, she was in disbelief, because she thought that because she was not a big, beautiful woman at 250 pounds, and was instead closer to the expected average weight for her height at 160, she was the most attractive. But not to this man, his new girlfriend was. To put it more blatantly in his own words, his ex-girlfriend was:

- not a giving person,
- not a caring person and
- extremely materialistic.

However, the ex-girlfriend didn't see this, all that she saw was the pretty factor (the "Finest"), which was in direct contrast to her "List": the items that she believed to be the winning combination in the Mating Game for guaranteed victory. HIS perception of beauty was different to that of the ex. His perception of beauty was a big, beautiful woman with personality and emotional compassion. That was exactly the opposite of who the ex-girlfriend was.

Women who can't learn from these experiences and instead want to compare themselves constantly to other women, with only negative objectives in mind, fall victim to the "winner's curse". That's when you push to win the Mating Game, even when it is not in your best interest to win. You strive not to lose by winning, but this kind of winning, always produces losing results. It's wasted energy and self-defeating to your long-term happiness.

If you look at the Mating Game with an open mind, you wouldn't get all mixed-up in the winning and losing of it. There aren't any losers; it just feels that way sometimes. Every go round on the Mating Game offers an opportunity to learn. Learn about yourself; learn about what is important to you. And if you do that, then every Game, whether it continues or not, will offer an opportunity for something better.

However, people who don't understand the elements of their list and attempt to find a person who values the same elements on his/her list ends up in a place I like to call the "Danger Zone." The Danger Zone is the place you go mentally, when you decide that you need to please someone else in order to reaffirm who you believe yourself to be. A woman in the Danger Zone who believes beauty is what it takes, needs for someone else to acknowledge that she is beautiful, in order for her to continue to believe it herself. A woman who believes that sex is the way to a man's heart, will stop at nothing sexually to grab any man or any other woman's man in order to reaffirm that she is sexy and desirable. A person in the Danger Zone needs for someone else to acknowledge his/her strengths in order for him or her to recognize that she/he has still got it. These are the people who brag about their volumes of lovers or about the numerous people that adore their beauty. The general belief is that "…that many people can't be wrong." These are the people who easily fall victim to being the other woman or the other-one man. To this individual, their new lover or adorer merely picked the better person. If not in the beginning, then in the end this person eventually becomes some other man or woman's problem. This individual is always looking for the next conquest. So…

Where Did that Hoochie Meet My Man?

What is the hot spot for women to meet, catch and frequently have sex with married or taken men?

Clubs? No, clubs are a staple spot, especially for younger players and even though sex clubs (clubs that have rooms for quick casual sex) are now openly in existence, they are still not the number one place to meet, catch and have sex frequently with married men.

Health Clubs? That's a good try. No, health clubs would be around the number two spot, and we all know why. What better place to shop for hot bodies, than at an open meat market, where what you see is what you get. Steam rooms and whirlpools (sometimes shared by both men and women) are great places to go get hot and sweaty and then go get hot and sweaty again. I think you know what I'm talking about. It definitely sheds new light on why guys religiously spend time at the gym. As one woman put it:

"I want a man that will work hard, break a serious sweat, then get up, take a shower, hit the gym, and go to work."

So, guess again. Grocery Stores? Well, this is a great place for women to meet men, but still it's not number one. Actually, this choice would probably be in third place as an initial meeting place.

So, where is the number one place to meet, catch and frequently sleep with a married man? You guessed it if you said, "at work". The stories are true!!

The stories I have been told read like an "XXX" rated soap opera. Not only are they having sex in every inch of the warehouse, plant or office, but they are sharing women. Switching them like they are nothing more than an old favorite jacket. And more than that, each guy to ride the love train (office mistress) is educating others to do the same. These days, along with the health plan, 401k and sick leave, his employment package also entitles him to a piece of ass from the company mistress. She's like a time-share. As soon as one person gets his fill of her, another new guy comes along to take his place. And what better way for a woman to make sure that the man has a job than to pick a man at work?

Come on now! What is the first question women usually ask or think when they are looking for a new man? You're being real if you said, "Does he have a job?" Well, it's guaranteed that all of these men have jobs. So, watch out ladies, if your man, husband or boyfriend is spending a lot of time at work or has developed an instant interest in working long hours to get that overtime, it may be that he doesn't have to go far from his desk to get a little sexual healing.

The Danger Zone

Judy was the pretty young thing at the plant and she was, in fact, the company's extra benefit. An equal opportunity lover, because she did not discriminate on any basis. More importantly, she was a freak. She lived alone, and she loved to walk around her apartment nude with red high heels, or so the rumor goes. After which, her male guests were encouraged to spank her and make it hurt, doing anything and everything...or so the rumor goes.

"Man she worked me out!" one man told me. The girl was freaky, although you would never have known it from how she looked at work. At work girlfriend was very conservative; for what, I don't know because everyone knew she was the freak of the week and an easy lay. Even the other employed women of the plant knew this. However, if you are thinking that these women would tell the wives of these men about their little side fling, you are dreaming. They were not trying to get fired because they stopped the bosses' sex show. Oh, hell, no! That was not happening. And who would have believed them anyway? Most women are either in denial or in divorce. Divorcing themselves of their feelings and emotions in order to make themselves numb to all that is happening and all that is about to happen around them. Are you thinking, "These men are married! They are suppose to LOVE their wives!" Well, I ask you...

What's Love Got To Do With It?

"Your happiness could be my happiness," is the motto of every mistress or second-tier girlfriend. "Allegiance to none" is where her loyalties rest. One minute she's asking him out for coffee!! ...and the next minute, with the minute man, ...well, we know what she's doing in that next 60 seconds, well at least the next 15 seconds.

She doesn't think about who she's hurting. That's not her concern; she doesn't care. All that matters is that she gets hers. The only time she will think twice or repent is if the takeover was unsuccessful, then she retreats and claims ignorance. It's not always an obvious candidate. During one radio show, a woman called in and explained how she fell into this role.

Caller: Anita, we had sex. Now he doesn't want to talk to me.

Anita: So, what happened?

Caller: Well, I'll admit it. I was kind of horny.

Anita: ...and?

Caller: This guy had been doing work for me. You know, around the yard. He just looked so good, Anita.

Anita: So, what happened?

Caller: Well, it had been hot, really hot outside and he'd been taking off his shirt while he was doing the yard, and I just thought, 'why not?'. So, I asked him over to my house for dinner, later that night. When I asked him, I felt a little embarrassed because I was thinking about eating but I wasn't thinking about food.

Anita: Well, so far, I'm not seeing a problem. This all seems like a 'good to go' situation, to me.

Caller: He's married.

Anita: Oh....

Caller: His wife was out of town for the week. I knew because, I made use of small talk as an excuse to get up close and personal, especially when his hot body was gleaming with sweat.

Anita: All RIGHT! Let's slow down a moment, and keep with the initial plan. So, tell me how this story ends.

Caller: Well, he came over. We had dinner and then we ate.

Anita: Okay, I think I get the picture. What happened the day after?

Caller: That night, after we had sex, he said he would call me later, but now it's been two days since we did the do and he has not called. So, now I'm feeling kind of cheap and used.

Anita: You feel cheap because he didn't respond like you thought he would, don't you? If he had been all over you the night after and the night after that, you would not be regretting this act at all, would you?

Caller: Well, I guess not...

Anita: Come on! Be honest. You wanted sex and that's what he gave you, sex. You expected lust to turn to love, but it didn't. So, now that the fun little ride only lasted one trip, you feel cheated because you wanted more than one round on the roller coaster of lust.

Caller: Well, I guess you're right.

You know I'm right! You can convince yourself that you are doing a married woman a favor by taking away her husband, but you aren't.

Sometimes a newly acquired mistress of fun will claim ignorance and a serious inability to make clear judgment due to an over abundance of liquor, like on a show I remember several months ago.

Mistress: I am so sorry, Janet. Your husband and I were alone together and ...well, we both were drinking that night. I just want to put this event behind us and still be your friend.

Wife: How many times have you been with my husband?

Mistress: Only twice, and we have not done it since.

Now, come on! I don't claim to know much about liquor and getting drunk, but I do know that every time I have gotten what people would call "drunk" I knew exactly what I was doing. I was just a little quicker to do it.

Only blackouts qualify for acting without knowing. But if you blacked out, you wouldn't be able to remember the act...right? So, these people who beg for forgiveness and REMEMBER the event, participated in the event willingly and knew what they were doing. But more importantly, if a person does it once and has the advantage of a previous event to warn him/her against doing it again, and he/she does it AGAIN...then that person did it willingly without exception.

The mistress who embarks on an unsuccessful takeover of another woman's man will even blame herself, although it's not sincere. Any and every effort to reclaim what she will potentially lose in the defeat of her ambush (of your man), is open to possibility. This is NOT repenting; this is DAMAGE CONTROL!! She will attempt to minimize her losses.

A potential fling (or flavor) of the month looks at people for the ways that they can supplement her/his life and her/his lifestyle: family, love, companionship, money, success, clothing, jewels, rent, vacations, etc. And just as she looks at her friendships as opportunities to get things, so does she in viewing her intimate relationships...

A mistress looks at a man and sees financial security, a better life, comfort, sex, stability, extravagance and a list of other things that do not include love. Oh, she's lovin' all right. She's lovin' his extravagance, his life and his money, but rarely does she ever love the person or the object of her affections.

She may call it love, but it's everything but. She is cold-hearted and empty: empty for many things that she has chosen you to provide for herself. She functions much like a parasite, feeding on someone else's bounty or horn of plenty. It's an exchange, a barter of sorts, but don't dare call it love; it's not love.

Have you ever defined love? Stop for a moment and answer the following question: When do you know you're in love? I asked 80 women this question. Simply translating their answers, they said that love was predominately:
- lust,
- security,
- passion and
- dependence.

One woman within the group openly said, "You're in love when you can't live without the other person."

Another woman jumped in with, "I don't think I've ever been in love, then because my answer is always 'yes'".

But that's not love, that's dependence: dependence on acceptance, money, emotional stability, aside of a few other things. We like to think that these items come free in a nice package called a husband, a wife, a boyfriend or a girlfriend, but they don't. Nothing is free. Everything has it's price. Even relationships come with a price tag. Don't for one moment think that it comes free, because…

You've Got to Pay to Play!

The Mating Game is a subsection of the Game of Life, the rules are very much the same. For example: Life is a very just creditor. It will take your payment in any form: years of despair, denial and regret. It will gladly take part of your youth, steal some of your hope and your drive and leave you high, dry and bitter.

It's like gambling in a Vegas casino; you know the odds are against you. You know that you're more likely to lose, but for some reason you always think that this spin of the wheel will be different. Constantly hoping for the next card dealt to be your jackpot, …your free ride, your easy street, or winning ticket to the good life. But each time you spin the wheel, you have to wager a bet or provide a small fee.

Sure, you get those free drinks, your temporary high, your momentary happiness, as long as you're spending, but as soon as the house cuts off your credit, it's a different game. Not only do you find yourself with nothing, but you may also end up in big debt. Debt that commonly comes with usury or death defying interest rate. However, unlike your student loans, every bill WILL be paid in full.

When that momentary good ride is over, you look back with the thought, "Well, it was fun while it lasted." However, with time, that sentence changes to: "How could I have been so STUPID?!" Somehow, no matter how many times you ask yourself the question, you will always find someone else as equally unknowing and willing as you were (and/or are now) to take your place at the game table. Someone younger, with more time to waste or burn and more credit to blow. That special someone is always willing to play the game, (the Mating Game) and take your spot to gamble at the Player's Table.

However, it's not until you leave the game floor for a time that you notice that the dealers are still playing the same game and the casino is still fixing the cards with the same tricks. No one can convince the new players that the game is fixed, because they think the games are new and merely requiring a higher level of skill, but it's a little more than that. The best player will always win and that's usually the person who has created the game. So, the dilemma becomes: to play, or not to play...that is the question. And if you do play, are you playing on your own terms? What do you demand & are you getting or just demanding? Some feel compelled to ask only for the minimum, like sex. So, do you proudly proclaim...

I'm Just Using Him For Sex?

Some female players (Player Penny's) say they're just in it for the joy of sex! Or as Digital Underground put it, "If you kiss me, then I'll kiss you back". Their belief is that you both gave each other something, it was mutual. I think you get the idea. One Penny, a 27-year old woman from Queens, New York said:

"I am sick of men thinking they are using me for sex. Hell, I'm using them for sex! How egotistical can you get? Those good looks are only good for 30 minutes, an hour if you're lucky. To fill my bed the requirements are just that simple. But to fill my heart, a man requires much more." said Tamesha 20 and still looking, as she put it. It's easy to find a quick lay in a club. He's looking. I'm looking. Men have said to me more times than not, 'If a woman wants to have sex, all she has to do is ask.' That could only be true if men are always willing. We know what the deal is before we said,

Hi....and there you have it." said Nancy a 29 year old sports writer."

Is it Really Your Idea?
"Whose idea is it anyway?"

The Power of Suggestion.
Shelia was an independent woman, doing well in every professional matter. However, she was not dating any one person seriously. She had been told on occasion that she was surrounded by nice guys that she simply discounted, by not giving them a real chance. So, Shelia decided to make an effort to look at her male friends and see if any of them had the qualities she valued and, in essence, deserved a more serious consideration as boyfriend material.

In looking at her pool of male friends, she noticed one that seemed to be doing well professionally, had a very pleasant attitude and was somewhat attractive. Keeping in line with her decision she personally confessed to herself that she should start looking at this male friend a little differently. She called up her good friend, Sara and in an evening conversation told Sara what she was thinking.

"He has a good job, he is a pleasant guy to be around, don't you think so, Sara?" Two nights later, Shelia gets a call from Sara.

"Shelia, um. I've been thinking about what you were saying, and if you aren't trying to kick it with him, I am."

This is the power of suggestion. Sara had not even thought twice about this guy, until Shelia introduced the idea to her, and two years later they are still together.

You might be thinking, "If a woman knows what she wants and decides to go for it, what's wrong with that? And if a woman is in it just for the sex what's wrong with that?" The answer is that only 10% of the women that said they were in it just for the sex, were.

That's scary! After talking to the other 90% of the women that claimed to be creeping purely for a good lay, I discovered that their reasons were twisted. What they were really looking for wasn't sex, it was love, family, husband, relationship, confidence, success, money, the joy of life, excitement, fun and the list went on to include anything and everything but love. This wasn't love; it was need dependence.

Again, you may be asking, "What's the problem with that?"

Well, if you convince yourself that you are looking for one thing and are really looking for another, what are your chances of finding it? And how long do you think it will take to find that something you are not even looking for? Lastly, during the time that you don't have this thing that you really want, how happy do you think you will be? These are the concerns.

Chapter 8

The Winners' Curse

■ ■ ■

In the course of playing The Mating Game, we want so badly to win that we either convince ourselves that a losing situation is a winning one or we convince ourselves that what we have is actually all that we need.

The Top 6 Reasons for Leaving a Relationship
"...and Cheating is NOT number 1...!"

We all want to think that cheating is the number one reason for leaving a relationship. We are so involved with this concept of cheating that we will not leave a clearly crappy relationship until we can CONFIRM that a man is cheating, but of the top six reasons there are five other more important reasons that should be stronger or more compelling reasons for leaving... and would not require a single piece of evidence of a cheating affair.

From the most important being number 1 to the least important being number 6, the top 6 reasons are:

1. *Physical or Emotional Abuse*
2. *Lack of Respect*
3. *Abuse of Trust*
4. *Lack of Life Contribution*
5. *Poor Communication*
6. *Cheating*

However, while these are issues that some people face, others just have other problems, like...

Emotional Disability.
How else could someone constantly form relationships, only to walk away like clockwork at the same point every time? This is similar to trying

to call someone only to get a busy signal every time. The person with an Emotional Disability, in that scenario, takes their phone off the hook, because they're not trying to hear you! People typically blamed for this problem are met in the earlier phases of relationship development, like the Hunt and Discovery. Although no one phase corners the market on this problem, it's just more visible at the earlier stages. How else could they be so detached, cold and unreachable? Emotional Disability! They don't feel, so they won't have to feel responsible, remorse or pain, when the time comes to walk away. They are aware of what is to come, the other person usually is not. So, they generally come off as cold, heartless and uncaring. The only thing worse than an Emotional Disability, is to be blinded by...

RCG Syndrome.

RCG Syndrome, also known as Rose Colored Glasses Syndrome, is when life is shitty and life continues to get shitty, because you pretend not to see your life situations for what they are. It's really not as simple as you might think. For a person experiencing RCG Syndrome, they usually explain it as simply a positive attitude. However, let me help you understand the difference.

A positive attitude is to know that your life has some shitty points but to remain positive, while you take steps to improve and correct those shitty points. RCG Syndrome is to see the shitty points; acknowledge the shitty points and then leave them untouched, only to let them get worse, because you convince yourself that those points aren't that shitty. That's the difference.

Now, whether a person is suffering from an Emotional Disability or experiencing RCG Syndrome, the question then becomes...why? Well, some suffer from being a prisoner of love, or as I like to call it...

Sex Slave:
Sex Dependent

Question: What does sex mean to you? If you couldn't have sex anymore, what would that mean that you were giving up?

When you think of dependence, you think of alcohol or drugs. Only recently have people begun to think of sex as an addiction, although the concept is certainly not new. Maslow defined a hierarchy of what he perceived to be the basic and essential needs of humans several decades ago; along with food and shelter, he also listed sex.

Women today are independent, making their own way, paying their own bills. So, what does a woman need a man for... The answer is "Sex!" It's one answer, anyway. It's one thing that she can't really give herself, excluding all battery operated items.

So, what happens? A woman meets a man. He doesn't have to have much. He doesn't need to have much. They go back to her place and POW! One good roll in the hay gives her a missing element of pleasure and excitement that she has not experienced in a long time. So, she keeps him on hold on the side. Every Tuesday or Friday, she calls him up, and he comes over to effectively do the do and he does and he is out of there.

Let's look at the entire picture now. He is the only one in her life giving her an item that she feels she needs. It is adding something to her life that she didn't have before. He is low maintenance. She starts a habit. He comes over all the time. What is the conclusion? She begins to expect it. She begins to crave her Tuesday or Friday night session. Is she going to give him up? No. Why would she. She hears from her girlfriends that he is creeping out in the streets with other women on Saturday night. Is she going to cut him loose? No. Why? Because she is addicted to his sex. She has become a sex slave.

What does sex mean to her? For some, getting sex means they're receiving companionship or love. For some women, experiencing sex means that they are voluptuous, desired or wanted. For some, sex means that for at least one moment they are not alone. For some, sex means that we have taken a step forward in a relationship. For others, sex is just a good time, similar to having a meal. Sometimes you like what you get. Other times you are just plain disappointed. Sometimes you walk away content and fulfilled. Other times, you look at the experience and think, "where's the beef?"

However, it takes an array of experiences to allow you to compare. Experiences in life are the basis of our growth. When we limit those experiences, we limit our ability to compare what is good to what is great, and what is okay to what really sucks. Just like Jenny...

It's All Relative...

Question: Have you had enough relationships and experiences to know what you want?

Jenny was a person who enjoyed working. Many people defined who she was by the quality of her work. As a result she didn't have much time for deep seeded relationships. As life would have it, she met a guy that didn't want to invest a lot of time in a relationship. He was attractive, but not the brightest light on the street. He couldn't really converse with her about the things that she enjoyed and they didn't really share any common interests. But he was pretty to look at, a bracelet (something pretty to hang on your arm that looks nice for everyone to see), and he was good in bed. So, she was okay that. It wasn't as though she was head over heals for him, but she thought he was fun and they had fun together.

After a while the relationship progressed, even though Jenny thought he was all right, but nothing she would write home to mother about. So, as things would happen, one date led to two and they eventually had sex. Now I'm going to get a little personal and tell you that, Jenny told me that when they had sex, sometimes she actually enjoyed it and sometimes she didn't, but Raymond, her boyfriend, appeared to be enjoying himself so much, that she just thought, "...if I give it a little time, maybe my enjoyment will just kick in."

Well, months went on and Raymond was having such a great time during their sexual escapades, that soon Jenny started to believe it too. Mind you nothing had changed. However, she had been told that most of sex is mental, and somehow she mentally convinced herself that she was enjoying these moments too.

After a while, Jenny told me that she began to expect Raymond to come over on a certain night of the week for them to have their weekly fling. I asked her why and she said that it was now something that she looked forward to.

Well, eventually, the relationship ran it's course and Jenny called me one night crying about how she had lost Raymond. She continued by saying that he was with someone else, she saw them. After listening to her for a while, I bluntly said to her in between the tears: "You are not crying because you lost Raymond. You are crying because you lost the game to someone else." She immediately stopped crying. I don't think that she consciously knew why she stopped crying so suddenly, but her subconscious mind knew. And it was because I had spoken the truth. She then thought about it for a while and admitted that I was right. It was a painful experience to feel that she was not the prize that she felt she was in Raymond's eyes, and it was a painful thought to feel a sense of loss for what she perceived to be a fundamental and basic need (through sex) that would now no longer be fulfilled.

Ironically, Jenny started dating other people and she found a new boyfriend shortly after her breakup with Raymond. Again, the relationship ran its course and they got to a point of becoming intimate and to Jenny's surprise the sex was GREAT! No, "...you don't understand, " as she put it: "When I was with Raymond, I thought the sex was great, but I just convinced myself of that. Of course, I didn't realize that I was glorifying okay-sex and mistakenly believing it was GREAT sex!" she said.

Well, the point here is that Jenny probably would not have ever known what she was missing, had Raymond not turned out to be such a jerk. Jenny then took it a step further and realized that she had in her mind glorified the sex and become a sex slave not because the sex was so great, but because of what she thought he and the sex brought to her life. Furthermore, Jenny denied herself several things. She had done so with the excuse that it was a sacrifice for something better tomorrow; like not going to parties when she was in college because she had to study constantly or like not going to happy hour when she was working because she could always make a report better by working later. So, as a result she felt alone and in large part that is what the sex brought to her life: the feeling that she was not alone. But that's not all.

Indirectly, Jenny had created holes in her life that she didn't even realize she had created. There was no fun, no excitement, no new experiences. And this is what her poor relationship unknowingly brought to her life and what she associated the sex with. In her mind, sex equated to all these essential things in her life, she could not break free. Not only was she a sex slave, but she was attached to her previous boyfriend due to a lack of experience in her relationships. This is why it is important to date several people before you become serious with one. You need some form of reference, something to compare your guy to. Getting serious with your first guy without past experience makes it hard to make an important decision such as marriage or commitment. Lastly, and importantly, she had grown attached to Raymond by what I call the Pretty Colored Chains.

Need Dependence

We value different things. Some women put a higher value on emotional support, whereas other women might place a greater value on sex or financial substance. It varies. The woman looking to creep is not always looking for money, but she is always looking for something of value, and what she really values depends on her needs and wants. This is what we refer to as need dependence. It's a concept that we have already briefly mentioned within the text of this book and is considered to be a pretty colored chain or a barrier to freedom.

I've already made reference to Pretty Colored Chains. These come in many colors to represent:

1. Good Sex
2. Romance
3. Friendship
4. Companionship
5. Positive Reassurance
6. Emotional Support
7. Comfort

And while these items appear to be golden, all that glitters, is not gold. In fact, much of what glitters like gold is actually fool's gold, an imitation with limited value. For this foolish substitute, we would and often times do trade our souls, only to find out later that what was received for a bargain was actually our time, our companionship, our youth, and our "assets". What we thought was so valuable that we were receiving for free, instead had a much higher fee than we could have imagined

Nothing comes free. If you read between the lines and the small print on the back of the contract before you signed, maybe you wouldn't be so quick to sign on the dotted line and become a...

Golden Girl: Need Based Chains

Question: If you had to leave your relationship right now, what would that mean you would be giving up? Would you be leaving an essential part of yourself behind?

Unknowingly Jenny was also a Golden Girl, a woman who was bound to a man because of the things that that man brought to her life. Although sex can be associated as a need that can produce a chain, it's not the sex that produces a dependence. It is what the sex REPRESENTS. However, a relationship does not need to include sex for a person to be bound by a Pretty Colored Chain. Chains are produced when the basic elements that are needed for one person to operate and function independently are coming from someone else (i.e.: a husband or boyfriend).

I refer to them as golden because we associate value to precious metals that are shiny, like gold. But a chain is a chain. If it were made out of plain metal, you wouldn't want it. But, because the metal is golden it becomes desirable and something that is something that we must have. As briefly mentioned earlier, pretty colored chains come in all colors. Therefore, having one doesn't necessarily stop you from wanting the others. The red shiny chain is so pretty (representing love) and the green shiny chain is so wonderful (representing money and financial stability). So, by the time, we get finished putting on at least one of every chain to supplement what we don't have in our own lives, we are...what? That's right. ...a Golden Girl.

Don't Touch My Chains!

I was watching an episode of Ricki Lake that was entitled, "Cheating Caught on Tape". Couples went on television with the prerequisite that the person in the relationship who was believed to be cheating had to work with a camera person and literally document the entire case to show exactly how they were cheating, step by step, in blow by blow detail.

Some of these cheaters were husbands cheating on marriages, others were simply significant others in supposedly monogamous relationships. You would think that by simply KNOWING that your spouse had AGREED to appear on a show called "Cheating Caught on Tape" would have been enough for these women (and men) to say, "Okay, he's cheating on me," and drop him on the spot! But it wasn't. Instead, these cheaters (men and one woman) smiled so proudly with such an extreme look of arrogance, that it became irritating.

There was a wife who was cheating on her second husband with her first husband (now her ex-husband). After her current husband saw her strip on tape along with the rest of the world for her EX-HUSBAND, you would think her current husband would have been FURIOUS. Instead, he said he was going to give her a second chance. He should have more appropriately called it her 22nd chance. Because he admitted that he knew that she was cheating with her ex long before the show. He admitted to that. He also knew how she was doing it (cheating). Her current husband had even picked up the phone once when her ex had called and had known about their method of paging to secretly contact one another...and you want to tell me this was her second chance with husband number two? No. This wife smiled despite being caught in a lie, but her current husband still didn't acknowledge it.

The second couple on the show was also a husband and wife team, but this time it was the husband that was cheating on the wife. Sadly enough, this was their second time on Ricki's show showing the world that her husband was a cheater and also his second time caught cheating on tape. The first time she saw the tape, she stayed with him. Now, she was back for the second show to see it AGAIN on tape. Incredible!

The experts came out and I was curious to see how they were going to handle this, because they had some real Golden Children up there holding onto their chains. So, they started talking about perception versus reality, and it was making sense, but it wasn't cutting to the core for these people. So what did the Golden Children do? They did as they always do. They got upset because someone was trying to touch their chains. If you think of it in terms of pictures, these experts were trying to help them take off the chains of the Golden Children (through verbal understanding) and these people got defensive and verbally fought back.

The attitude is always, "How dare you touch my chains! In fact, these aren't even chains. They are a beautiful set of bracelets." You think I'm lying? Well, I really wish I was. These Golden Children waited for some word that they could jump on to attack the two experts' explanation of them. Finally, they found a word to jump on. When they said, "This isn't love," the two wives, stood up and said: "Love? YES, I love him! The only reason I'm with him is LOVE!" Then the two wives high fived each other. This was done right after Jenny (one of the two wives) said... she was going to leave her husband.

Yep, sure you are...Jenny. Guess her conviction to leave her husband didn't mean anything. Then again, why should it? It didn't mean anything the first time either. So, what happened? Well, several things, but let's start with that word love. Remember these two women jumped on the first word they could to defend their cheating spouses. Why? Because, if there is something wrong with him, then there is something wrong with her for staying with him, for believing him, and with her judgment in believing him for this long. The best way to protect against all of these doubts is to simply, believe him (or her) again. That cuts out all the potential pain that could come with one simple act of leaving (or taking off Rose Colored Glasses). So, women bend over backwards and refuse to admit to the reality of a cheating relationship, because the fear of losing even the little bit of affection, the little ounce of companionship, the little teaspoon of loving, would take away from the BASIC amount that she needs just to survive. Remember she is supplementing her low levels of these pieces in her life with a few golden chains from him. So, until she acknowledged the chains that bind, these chains will continue to blind. However, more simply put, the pain associated with leaving him is far greater than the pain of believing that he cheated and wants to make it right by staying in the relationship.

A Higher Tolerance For Pain.

See, everyone watching a talk show wants to see that happy ending occur before the end of the show. The sad reality is that people don't leave a relationship or a sad way of life until they are ready to do so. Sometimes it takes a pain so great, so unbearable that change is not even an option, it's a mandatory requirement. The concept of watching your husband boldly cheat before your very eyes on tape was obviously intended to bring forth a pain so hurtful that it would induce change. But people can be trained to endure a higher tolerance for pain. It was obvious that that was what had happened to those people. Do you actually think the cheating spouses would have allowed their cheating process to be taped, if they didn't already know that the tolerance level of his or her spouse was prepared to endure it? No, they wouldn't have. These cheaters had already trained their spouses and lovers to endure a much higher level of pain and discomfort in a relationship than anyone (watching the show) had anticipated. Diaries, video tapes, verbal confessions ...it didn't matter. They knew their spouses were bound to them by their Golden Chains and weren't going anywhere. When the PERCEIVED value of what a cheating man brings to the table is greater than the anticipated pain of leaving, the Golden Child will always choose to stay.

People can be trained in a few ways to have a higher tolerance for pain. First, it can be that they were taught that a higher level of abuse (mental and/or physical) was acceptable by watching Mommy and Daddy. Dad fought; Mom accepted the blows. Dad cheated; Mom pretended not to know. Children watch, learn and believe that the way it is at home is the way it is suppose to be.

Secondly, women can be beaten down to constantly want less, until what they perceive to be acceptable is what he is willing to give. Give an inch, he'll take a yard. Women that consistently don't stand their ground on their standards, constantly allow their standards to be lowered until anything goes. When that happens, he knows that she is now prepped for anything: cheating, abuse, video tape, etc. Anything goes at that point. And that's what the cunning little smile meant on the faces of these men on this show as they quietly grinned after they once again said, "I'll stop cheating."

All That Glitters Is Not Gold

Pretty Colored Chains are need-based chains that come connected to a person.

A couple of years ago, I went on a talk show and met a well-dressed, attractive, seemingly intelligent woman who had a beautiful little boy. This woman then went on the show to tell everyone on national television that her husband kicked her in the stomach while she was pregnant, was cheating on her, and was openly beating her. When I asked her, "Knowing all of this, why are you staying with him?" She replied, "...because I love him."

If I could erase two phrases from the English Language, I would get rid of "low self-esteem" and "I love". Both are used when people can't explain or don't know what the HELL they are talking about! They are catch all phrases that qualify, can and have been used to explain EVERYTHING...but usually mean NOTHING.

Love is a word that represents the unexplainable to most. So, when we have emotions or attachments and can't explain what they are, we jump on the love train with everyone else and call it "love". But most every time, it's not love, it's need, and these are the Golden Children who were the "Pretty Colored Chains".

So, when we take the pretty colored chains and feel that our needs have been fulfilled with a quick fix, by taking some of someone else's (love, comfort, security, etc.) or vibing off that person's stability or joy we quickly call it "love". However, when that happens, you have nothing more than a short-term fix. Now, you're an emotional junky and a slave to need or are need dependent. You've lost the most valuable ability that you've got in crafting or finding a strong relationship, and that is the ability to walk away...permanently.

On a talk show a year ago, I met with 8 couples. What I found interesting was that all of the women claimed to be committed to a relationship that their boyfriends or husbands claimed would never work or was absolutely over. What made them so interesting was the way the producer had placed them on the stage. She had put the most obviously hopeless case on the far left and placed the woman that appeared to have all the self-confidence in the world on the far right. In between were shades of gray that slowly moved from one hard extreme to the other.

The funny thing was that all of these women had hopeless relationships. The woman who appeared to have all of the confidence in the world was hopelessly in love with a gay man. I didn't say bi-sexual, I said gay. Therefore, unless this man decided to change his sexual preference, she should not expect to see a ring on her finger anytime in the near future or ever.

The woman that everyone appeared to identify with was financially independent. She dressed well; she was well spoken and seemingly confident, but the truth was that she was the same as the woman at the other end of the row (the opposite extreme) whose husband beat her and who didn't even attempt to raise her voice to him. I know what you're thinking. You think I have lost it, but you will understand that I am right in a moment, just stay with me on this.

It was so easy for everyone to point the finger at the lady on the other end who was obviously in a bad relationship and say: "See, I know what a bad relationship looks like. It's YOURS and I know that I would never put myself into a situation like that! God knows, I would never stay in a relationship like yours. You should leave him!"

About this time, the entire audience stood up in applause to attempt to coax this very same woman into leaving her husband. The very same woman who had just told everybody that she had been in this bad relationship as a battered wife for 10 years. Still, they stood to attempt to, somehow, help her find some new revelation within herself and tell her prison-warden-husband who owned all the chains she wore to, "Go to Hell because she's leaving, today!" But while everyone was thinking about her long-term future in her making this one decision, I was thinking about her immediate future in making this one decision.

The sad truth was that if she didn't understand why her current relationship was bad and why she should get out in the first place, the probability of her accepting her husband back or getting back into a relationship just like the one she was leaving (if she decided to leave at that moment without that understanding) was extremely high. It's like making the same mistake twice, without stopping to re-evaluate what your initial mistake was to begin with. This could be equated to a person who constantly puts her hand back into the fire only to be burned over and over and over again. She experiences pain, but does not see or connect the logic or error in her judgment that led to her hand getting burned.

So, what made these two women of extreme's on the show similar? They both wore Pretty Colored Chains and the Pretty Colored Chains were the ties that bound them to their men. Now, the woman with the poor self image wore more Pretty Colored Chains than the woman at the other end, but never the less, they both wore chains. Also both allowed themselves to continue to be in these relationships as a result.

Granted, there are some relationships that are abusive and require a special or planned effort to leave; however, many women are not a part of that category; instead, these women allow themselves to be bound by these self-induced chains. The unbelievable fact is that women could take these chains off if they truly wanted at anytime; however, many decide not too. Why? Because their fear of the known is less than their fear of the unknown. This is, of course a matter of perception, because the true reality was that the future offered unlimited possibility, while the past provided known limitations, which brings me back to the second word I would strip from the English Language, "low self-esteem".

Again, I really hate the phrase "low self-esteem", because it implies that you have no sense of self worth at ALL. When it's used on people, these individuals jump to their own defense, because to be told that you have "low self-esteem" is an insult. Therefore, by using this phrase you have not only insulted the person you were intending to help, but you have also alienated them by putting them on the defensive. At that point, you can believe they will not listen to another word you have to say. So, the use of the phrase is a mistake. It's also a catch-all phrase that has been used over and over again to explain something that people don't understand clearly. So, it's an overused word and overused words lose their value, meaning and impact.

What a person means and should say instead is, that the individual has "low confidence in their ability to repeat their successes": such as find another boyfriend who has at least the basic minimum standards as the one she's currently with. The fear is always that she will go backwards, that she will end up with less or nothing. That's fear.

Now, the woman with the supposed self-confidence wasn't any better or any different from the woman at the other end, no matter how much she wanted to believe it, and that is what professional women need to understand. Just because you have the financial stability chain covered doesn't mean that you can't get pulled in and led to put on a pretty colored chain of a different color: affection, comfort, emotional support.

Dana was beautiful. She was a District Manager for a top computer company in the Midwest and she was doing well. With an excellent education, great salary and respect from her co-workers and friends, it would be easy to believe that she had it all. So, what was her problem? Dana was chained by the pretty red colored chain that represented sex and companionship. She met this guy who really shared no common interests with her, but he gave good sex, and she was happy with that. She was also afraid of being alone, so that made it difficult to leave without having someone else in a ready-to-go mode. So this guy moved in, she paid all the bills, and he gave her good sex every night when she got home. But Dana traveled a lot due to her job which left the door open for live-in lover to play, when the cat was away.

What's wrong with that, you might ask? They were both consenting adults, right? Well, the problem is that when she was in town, she didn't go out to meet other people. So, in a way, Dana didn't explore the opportunity to meet other people that might have had more in common with her than her present lover. Therefore, she just settled for the relationship she had. Of course, her lover said that he was committed to her but he wasn't, despite their arrangement. He was seeing other women in her house, in her bed, with her money and in her car, but no one would tell her about it and if they did, she would not have believed it because she said they had a relationship built on trust (a preferred weapon used in the Mating Game, as discussed previously in the book).

As we've discussed, needs come in an assortment of colored chains: affection, sex, companionship, money, comfort, supplementary success, family, security, fun, emotional stability, confidence and support. For some women, even if you already have some of what the chain offers, you can never have too much of a good thing!

Too Much Is Never Enough

The truth is that more and more women are becoming mistresses or content to be the other woman. Why? Because although they have some money, financial or even emotional stability of sorts, they desire more or desire to improve upon what they do have. However, a mistress doesn't just desire more. A mistress covets.

Just as Hannibal Lector so eloquently said in the movie, *Silence of the Lambs*: "We covet and want what we see every day." So the mistress not only wants more, she covets what she perceives as someone else's happiness, someone else's value and someone else's more.

So, let's turn the tables for a moment. Let's imagine that you have decided to go clubbing. You find some guy. You both get together. Sex is great. The following day, things just aren't going right; in fact, they aren't going at all. He breaks it off. Aside of what we've learned from in the beginning of the book, what happened! What went wrong? Let's look at some of the possibilities.

If You're Selling, I'm Buying!
Question: Do You Know What You Are Offering?

One of the most commonly asked questions by both men, as well as women is: Why are the people I date always after one thing? The answer is easy: "if you're selling, they're buying." What that means is, that if you present yourself one way, people assume that that is who you are and make their decisions based on that understanding. So, in an indirect weird kind of way, the person who presents themselves wrongly is in part responsible for not ending up with the type of person they wanted. So, if a woman comes to a club wearing a dress so tight that she's afraid to breathe for fear of a unsightly bulge appearing at the tummy line, she should not be surprised if men approach her for sex. Why? Because, "if you're selling, he's buying".

Likewise, if you're a man and you approach a beautiful woman and tell her all about your new Mercedes, your 6-figure job and your penthouse apartment, do not be surprised if she wants you for your money. Why? Because that's what you were selling and that's what she was buying. So, if you don't want to pickup a woman that wants you solely for the things that you can give her or if you don't want a man who is only interested in having a relationship with you for all of 10 minutes, "you need to come to that person "correct," honest and up-front!" So, think about what you're selling and remember, if you're selling, I guarantee somebody will be buying.

    A word to the wise: if you decide to play this game of charades despite the warning, beware. Ladies, you might meet a man who appears to be your dream come true, just as you appear to be his. So, you sex him up. Three weeks later you discover that his car was leased, his clothes were rented and his penthouse was a house-sitting gig. But you aren't any better, because you know your hair was purchased, your figure is courtesy of a Frederick's of Hollywood foundation garment (a girdle) and your car was on loan from your girlfriend. (Smile.) You both just got "tricked"! You tricked each other for sex and a fake moment. Remember an important rule of the game: play and be played.

Giving Him A Piece.

    When you give a man a "piece of ass" (sex), is that all that you are giving him? When you give a man a look, a stare and a flirtatious "piece of leg" (tease), is that all you are giving him? I don't think so. Do you know what you are giving? Because a piece of leg (simple flirting) turns into a piece of ass (sex). You then get upset and feel cheated, so you give him a "piece of your mind" (verbalize your pain) because you're pissed at yourself that you gave him a "piece of your heart" (your love and devotion). So, you stay with him because you can't move on and you pay the ultimate price by becoming his long-term servant and give him a "piece of your life" (irreplaceable time).

People will take whatever you give them, and women have been naive enough to give it all to whomever is willing to take it. But not all women who willingly give up a part of themselves do it unknowingly...

Coochie Under Contract

"A man doesn't have to be rich to have a woman at his beck and call," claims an unknown voice trying to change the more popular concept. "A mistress is not a woman of luxury, she is a woman of convenience". Beverly from Colorado continues the thought "...Or as I like to call it, Coochie Under Contract!" Married or not, single or divorced, it doesn't matter anymore, if it ever did.

"I usually date 2 men at a time" Jessica said. Of course that would not normally be an issue. However, the fact that Jessica was married made it an issue. "I would rotate them every 4 or 5 months, depending on how things went. But when I met Eric, I stopped looking. We've been seeing each other now for about a year and a half."

That would not be a problem if Eric was the name of her husband! Eric continues on, "Jessica is sweet. Sexually, she's got it going on and we're happy."

When I asked them if they wanted to get married, they quickly jumped in with, "Why spoil a good thing?" and laughed. "When I married my husband," Jessica continued, "he was independent, and a dreamer with a job. He had a lot of pluses. But when we got married, it was like he just shut off. Everything that he was, everything that he was striving to become, he slowly stopped going after. He just changed and became dependent on me."

Dependence is definitely a trait that leaves you needy, scared and desperate. They say that when animals get scared they release a sent that is known as the smell of fear, and fear becomes a scent that animals that prey on victims can smell.

You Think A Dog Can't Smell That!

Question: Are you secure and confident with yourself, or are you desperate to have someone in your life and fear the prospect of being alone?

How many of us have seen a beautiful woman with an ugly ass man? Ugly in appearance, ugly in attitude, just overall ugly. I have and I don't know how many times I've been disgusted by it. The woman is usually gorgeous, nice but something is always missing. The docile ones are easy to spot. If she is subservient, catering to his every whim, whatever he says is gold. We look at that and say: "What! Look at that girl! She's got low self-esteem." Don't we? (There's that phrase I hate again: "low self-esteem".) Okay. Let me give you another example:

A beautiful woman, let's call her Tonya. Fairly attractive guy, let's call him John. Both are dressed to the 9's. They walk into a club. They both have lots of personality. He finds her a seat and goes to get her a drink. Tonya smiles and spots one of her girlfriends who comes over to her table to sit down and talk for a while. John walks to the bar, asks the bartender for 2 drinks, spots a beautiful woman at the other end of the bar. This new woman's boyfriend is in a discussion with several male buddies.

The lady at the bar smiles at John. The bartender brings John his 2 drinks, and John asks the bartender what the young lady is having at the end of the bar. John tells the bartender to put her drink on his tab gives the bartender one of his business cards to be passed onto the young lady. The bartender takes the drink and the card and tells the young lady that the drink is from the man at the other end of the bar. John smiles. She smiles back, nods and puts the card in her purse. The lady then takes a sip. Her boyfriend swings around. The young lady tells her man that the bartender is still making his drink and he is none the wiser. John casually walks back over to his table, with his two drinks.

Now. What's your first thought? It's probably something like.. "That dirty dog!" Right? Or, "that hootchie, bitch!" Right?

What if I told you that John's girlfriend (Tonya) had suspected him of wrong doing for a while now, but was unsure?

What if I told you that Tonya had caught John doing this once before, but he had promised not to do it again?

What if I told you that she caught him dropping numbers to women a couple of times before this?

Why am I asking all of these questions? Because I want to know how much it would take before you would point the finger at Tonya. Are you shocked or surprised, that I am even making the statement? Well, let's touch on your answer. Did you at any point decide that Tonya was in some way responsible for staying in a relationship that did not grant her some respect? It's obvious that she was one of many. Did you think that Tonya was responsible after the second question? What about after the third? Most people would claim that she was responsible after the last question, because she "didn't know". "It's not fair to blame her, if she wasn't sure. But after she knew, then she allowed herself to be tricked" said 24-year old Angie. Most women think that way, but the question is "When did Tonya know?" Or better yet, "When did Tonya admit to knowing?"

The truth is that Tonya knew she was not the only one long before she verbally admitted to anyone that she merely suspected. All right. Now that we know that she knew she was not the only woman in his life and stayed, in spite of it, can you tell me why she stayed? I bet your going to say low self-esteem. But how can you say that? She obviously was very attractive, she had personality, she was making some good money because she could afford to dress well, so why would a woman who could have several men, stay with one man and be content to be one of many?

Sex? Sometimes, and sometimes not? So, what was my answer? My answer is that if you said that Tonya and the female at the bar were staying in their respective relationships for the same reason, you would be correct. So, what's that reason? Security and confidence, a lack of it! The thing that kept Tonya in a knowingly bad relationship and what made the second woman hold onto her existing boyfriend was security in knowing you've got one person there always, despite how crappy he may be. Despite it all, you're not alone, and that was what she feared, being alone; he knew that. He could smell that.

Secondly, what made the woman at the bar make an advance toward Tonya's guy? And what made Tonya stay despite what she knew was a lack of confidence in her ability to have a successful long lasting relationship with one guy? One decided to blindly accept (ignore) while the other decided to make the first move toward cheating to avoid being the person being cheated on.

Some people get their sense of value and worth from their accomplishments, others from their abilities. And taking a man from another woman is an ability. What I'm trying to show you is that confidence is segmented. I like to refer to them as the Categories of Worth.

The Categories of Worth.
Your life is divided into categories that you enjoy. If you have a job, then you have a segment in your mind that represents your professional success. If you enjoy some type of sport or hobby, then you have a segment mentally that represents your sports/hobby success. And like wise, you have a segment that represents your ability to socialize and again another one that represents your intimate relationships. Your confidence in your ability to repeatedly have successful outcomes is dependent on the number of successes and failures you have in each category.

For instance, if you have had several salary increases from your job and have received constant positive feedback from your supervisor then your confidence in your ability to repeatedly have positive outcomes in your performance would be high. However, if you have had more failures than successes in your intimate relationships, then your confidence in your ability to reproduce positive results in this category would be low. That's when you become vulnerable to fear and allow yourself to stay in relationships that hurt you or that stop you from being happy.

Chapter 9

Winning Ways

■ ■ ■

Don't Plug into my Power Strip!
Question: When you get involved in a relationship, do you change and become more dependent?

There is a misconception that when the wedding is over, the game is won. Well, we are finding out that this is not true. But in the process, women are plugging into someone else's power strip. What does that mean? Well, it is like Jeremy said. When he and his wife got married, she had a separate personality, her own goals and a life. When she married him, she stopped growing and started sponging off his vibe, his zest for life. In essence, she unplugged her power strip and became dependent on his power strip (of outlets).

What's wrong with that? Well nothing, if Jeremy had a lot of room (outlets) on his power strip. But the average guy has a few outlets and from his perspective, part of getting married is to increase the number of outlets, in order to have more of everything in life (more things working, more things going on). However, some women don't see it that way. When a woman gives up her power strip, of course, she's got to plug those appliances in somewhere; so she becomes dependent on him and this is one of the do knots of the Mating Game. That's why it's important to...

Know What You're Getting

Question: When you consider a guy as a potential boyfriend or husband, do you thoroughly examine who he is, inside?

You Better Shop Around.

Do you do your own shopping? Have you ever walked into a grocery store, gotten your basket and walked around getting items in the general area of the item that you needed? This would be like, knowing you need coffee. So, you walk over to the coffee section and without looking, you pull a container of coffee off the shelves and put it into your cart. You know it's coffee because the entire aisle of items is coffee, but you don't know what kind, what brand, what price, what size, what flavor or if it is decaffeinated or not. But, you know it's coffee. So, you're going to get it. Then you know you need some vegetable oil. So, you walk over to the place in the market, where there is an entire section devoted to cooking oil and you really don't look, you just pick one off the shelf and put it in your basket. Now, you don't know if that oil is vegetable, sunflower, olive, favored with garlic, basil or hot peppers. But you know it's oil. So you do this with the rest of the list of items that you need and you get to the cash register and you tell them to ring it up. You don't look at what you got, the price, or anything. You just tell the cashier to ring it up and bag it. Now you get home and your goal was to have a cup of coffee and a slice of cake.

Well, when you open up the bag, you discover that you don't have anything you can use for what you wanted. The coffee is decaffeinated and the brand you hate, so you don't want that. And the oil you got is some kind of substitute soybean stuff flavored with oregano; you can't use that to make a cake. You have just wasted all of your time, effort and money. You don't have anything that you can use and you know that on top of it all, you've got to go back to the store again because you still need those items.

You may think all that waste was silly but isn't it the same thing to find a guy and get married, while not having asked the important questions that can affect your life? Don't you think it is important to know if he wants to immediately have 5 children or wait and adopt 2? That could be a problem for you if you just got that new promotion. He may want to move to Kansas because it is his life-long dream, but Kansas is just not the same as California, the place you've always wanted to live.

Oh, you are probably thinking, "Of course, I asked all the questions I needed to, I know exactly who he is, and did all of my investigating before I got into this game." Oh, really, what about the questions you needed to ask yourself?

- Was he a player before you met him?
- If he was, are you sure he isn't now?
- Was he controlling before you got married?
- If he is controlling, do you think he's going to tighten or loosen his grip of control after the wedding?
- Is he capable of abuse: mental or physical?
- Has he been abusive before?
- How does he handle his temper?

How do you think abusive relationships start? Could yours be one? He says he wants to have a baby with you, how is he treating his other children and the mothers of his existing kids? Do you think this time will be any different? The odds are against you that his past actions will not be repeated. Who he is, is who he is. Just as, who she is, is who she is.

Go Inside The House.
I met a young woman, in Georgia a few years ago. She seemed very sweet and she was young. We met after I did a seminar. We sat down and she started talking about her boyfriend who was into questionable criminal activity. She was young, couldn't have been anymore than 19. She told me that she was expecting a child and was several months into the pregnancy.

Listening to her speak, she was saying that when she first met this guy (Derrick), he was kind and sweet. They talked about having a family together, so she got pregnant and things started to change. They talked about getting married, but then he started becoming the complete opposite of who he was originally.

I looked at her and immediately thought of a first time home buyer who is so excited to go buy a house. Imagine this for a moment. A first time female home buyer goes out with a Realtor to look at homes and sees a house that is absolutely gorgeous! It is the epitome of what she has always wanted and all of this she gets from standing outside looking at the front of this house.

The Realtor then says to her, "Would you like to go inside it?"

She says, "No. I'll take it!"

The Realtor says, "Are you sure you don't want to see the inside of the house?"

And she replies, "No. It is exactly what I have always wanted. I'll take it!"

So, she pays her money, the full asking price of the house (no price negotiation necessary here), she signs on the dotted line and the house is all hers. She has her boxes packed and ready to move into her new beautiful home. Straight from closing the sale and getting her keys, she goes to the house with a truck full of her possessions ready to move in that very day.

Well, when she gets there, she tries using the key and notices that she is having a little bit of a problem opening the front door to the house. She continues and finally gets the door open. What does she find? The entire inside of the house is covered in dust and spider webs. No one has been inside for quite some time. There is broken wood all over the place. The ceiling needs patching because there is water damage all over. From one end of the house to the other, this place needs serious work. She thought she had bought a beautiful house in move in condition. What happened here? The same thing that happened to this woman who was sitting in front of me. She saw this guy and much like the woman that made the decision to buy the house by just looking at the outside, so did this woman in deciding to make a commitment of a child and pending marriage without knowing what she was getting into with this man.

In the beginning, this guy wined and dined her and she thought he was perfect. She didn't bother to try to find out more about him outside of what he allowed her to see, much like the woman standing in front of the house. Just as with our story, when she asked him personal questions, he would always change the subject. She had a hard time getting him to open up. Much like the door that wouldn't open to the front of the house; it would eventually. It just required a little more effort and time. If she had done the same with Derrick, she would have seen that her guy was a fixer-upper. He had a lot of things to work out in his own mind. He couldn't work through them alone, so that's why he got involved in this illegal activity which represented the water damage in the house scenario that needed to be repaired, but instead was damaging the house even further. Her problem was that she didn't take the time to find out what her guy was about and who he was: problems, imperfections and all. That's what happened here. She was without a doubt, emotionally attached to someone she didn't know.

Ignoring The Third Eye

Question: Do you openly evaluate your relationships, taking into consideration the worst as a possibility?

How many times have you seen a friend in a relationship with problems that were extremely obvious to you, but completely unknown to her? Tens of times, I'm sure. Why? Because it's always easier to see someone else's problems.

She can be in the exact SAME problematic situation and call someone else's exact same problem out in a second, but not see the very same problem that is going on in her own life. Why? Because we tend to ignore our third eye. What is the third eye? Some call it intuition, some call it a feeling. I like to refer to it as an actual eye that cannot be seen but that can instead be used, to see. However, instead of leaving it open all the time, we close that eye to avoid putting ourselves into painful situations, and open it to see the situations of others. This is a waste and a mistake. (Some people think that only women have this ability, but men do too.)

If you still don't know what I am talking about, think about a talk show. Pick anyone of them television or radio. They all will prove my point. Chances are greater than not that you will look at the people in the problematic situation and say, "I can't believe that person doesn't see that she needs to leave him!" Or, "I can't believe he is still with her!" I always find that funny, because we all know that despite the fact that we want to look at the people on the screen and say that he or she is an extreme case, we know that their are many people like them sitting at home saying the same thing and a good number of them are in a similar problem, just at varying degrees of severity.

For some reason, in our minds, we like to point out the extreme cases and say, "Look at that person, I sure don't have problems like that!" ...but we do. We do the same thing with soap operas. Despite what is going on in our lives, we like to look at those soap operas and say, "...at least my life is not that messed up!" But sometimes it is.

With millions of people watching the talk shows daily, we know that a good portion of the people sitting at home are in the same situation. We want to believe we are not, but many are. The only difference is the intensity of obviousness. I can say this because I've known many of them and a long while ago, I was one of them too. That's how I came to discover the third eye.

I don't discard those previous experiences as having been stupid or brush them off by claiming ignorance. Instead, I like to think that I traded them in for something more important: experience that I then converted into some level of wisdom, for better future decisions.

So, the final word is that using the third eye to view your own circumstances may initially be painful, but it is a saving grace in revealing the proper direction that should be taken in your life now, instead of 10 years and a withered spirit later.

Do Onto Others As You Would Have Them Do Onto You

Question: Do you use people in relationships or do you keep them around longer than you should for reasons that are exclusively self-serving?

I'm really not trying to get into anything religious, and you may think I'm weird by saying this, but it has been my experience that, what you do to others is done onto you, later if not at that exact moment, for both good and bad.

If you still don't believe my theory, here's another situation. A few years ago, a friend of mine named Janet had been dating this guy, Anton, for 3 years. She use to keep him on the side, ...for sex, she would say. She didn't really like Anton, not enough to keep a relationship going. She had told me that when she initially met Anton, she immediately thought, "I wouldn't really marry this guy". However, despite, the fact that she really did not take Anton seriously, she continued to date him. Now, I can understand dating someone for fun, but don't pretend that it is more than it is and keep someone on hold for 3 years. Never the less, that's exactly what Janet did.

I viewed Anton with my "third eye" and saw dead weight holding Janet down from finding someone else, but needless to say, she didn't see it that way.

"He's fun.." she would say. "He takes me out and we go places."

Janet had told me that Anton had in fact hinted that he might propose to her. I asked her what she was thinking about doing if he did ask, and she indirectly said that she had hinted back that it would not be a good idea for him to ask her right now. But despite that, Janet would not budge on making a decision to either move forward with him or to let him go and more forward without him. She saw him as her fun guy (a Fun Phil). He was good for her ego.

"I'm just using him for SEX!" she would jokingly say to me.

Well, around year 4, Janet called me crying. I asked her what was wrong. She said that she had just called Anton at home and some woman had answered the phone. When she asked Anton who it was, he said it was a friend who was staying with him temporarily. Janet eventually called back two more times to find that same woman there.

In the end, Janet discovered that this person was not just a friend, she was the woman whom Anton had been living with for the last 3 months. When Janet finally confronted both Anton and his live-in lover, Anton finally admitted that he had been unfaithful to Janet and actively dating other women for the entire 4 years.

Janet thought she was just using Anton for sex. Well, Anton was just using Janet for sex. Janet thought she was just keeping Anton around as a play thing. Well, Anton was just keeping Janet around as a play thing. When Janet finally opened her third eye, she realized that the times that Anton had mentioned marriage to her were just because he knew she would not say "yes" and were used in effect to keep her emotional state in check and under his control; Janet was a Dominant Donna. As long as Anton let her believe she had it under control, she was satisfied and left things alone. And that is why Anton had attempted to propose to Janet, it was a control measure. Janet thought the fact that he had proposed to her meant that he was under HER control. Ironically, it was his method of keeping her under HIS control.

When it was over, she realized that she had just wasted 4 years of her life pretending. She now saw that Anton had indirectly become a weight that kept her from experiencing new things, stopped her from growing personally and from potentially finding someone that she truly enjoyed spending all of her time with, not just some parts.

The bottom line is that Janet had been rawly used, in the same manner that she had used Anton. So, are you willing to pay the price, when the stakes are high? Or do you know when to stop betting?

Place Your Bets!

When you're young, you think you have time on your side and years to just give away. Don't you? Janet was 22 when she started playing the Mating Game and was 26 when she stopped playing at the same table with the same player. I wrote about her experience in my previous book. The piece was called, "I Got A Man". It was meant to be sarcastic, since she actually had very little of him, but she thought she did.

Ironically, Janet's replacement, Anton's new live-in lover, was a young 22 year old woman with most of the same traits as Janet. Anton found a new player for his table.

Young women think they have lots of years to bet with; they are such willing prey and such easy targets for an experienced player to use. These players, men and women, will suck the life blood out of you, if you are not looking, much like a "Gigolo Vampire" (a player with the experience to extract your youthful essence). But in reality women are giving away their youth, their time and their zest for life.

You Broke the Contract

Question: Is it your plan to change who you are if this round at the Game table goes well, and if so, have you communicated this to your lover yet?

I had a guy call into my radio show one evening. He was telling me how he found this wonderful woman. She was independent, doing her own thing, and had a lot going on. So much so, that he married her, but after they got married, things started changing.

He said that she quit her job without talking to him about it. She gave up working on her doctoral degree, which was one of her passions and she went from being a person with a busy agenda to a person with no drive that sat at home watching television and eating chocolates. He then confessed that she didn't even look the same anymore. She was once slender and trim, not anymore. She changed from a person who went to the gym twice a week to a couch potato whose only use of the word "gym" came right before the word Beam (Jim Beam) her favorite liquor. All of this led to her adding 40 pounds to her weight.

Caller: This is not the woman I married!

Anita: Have you told her any of this, Chris?

Caller: Of course, I hinted toward telling her these things, but...Hell! You know there is only so much that you can tell a woman before she thinks you are just being negative.

Anita: So, what are you doing about all of this?

Caller: I've tried. I've talked to her. I've tried to make her understand, but she just says I'm being insensitive. But, Anita, I didn't marry the woman that she is. She has completely changed and not for the better. I didn't buy into staying with this.

Anita: Chris, what are you trying to tell me? Are you seeing someone else?

Chris: Yes!

Anita: For how long?

Chris: Since the change got out of hand. But, Anita, I don't feel responsible. She broke the contract! I didn't buy into this.

Sometimes we pretend to be someone that we think people will want, but then when the real person comes out (the person that you are or that you want to be), others feel cheated. Why? Because you sold them on one person, then when you closed the deal, you did a switch to another person. Don't get me wrong. Maybe girlfriend is unhappy, but that doesn't make much sense. Because if they get married, and that was the very thing that she wanted, then that should be the happiest time for her life. Right? Wrong? Instead she changed right after the wedding. Men call this breaking the contract. So what is the answer? Don't pretend! You are who you are and if the person you are with cannot appreciate that person, then you are with the wrong man.

He Hit Me!!

Question: Do you punish your man by refusing to have sex?

I'm sure you think that this heading is extremely childish! Well, it was intended to be. How many women have said, "We had a disagreement; he was acting stupid; so, I punished him by not having SEX!" I hope you think that that statement is just as childish as the heading. It is always amazing to me how a woman can be in a committed relationship and think that she can regularly punish her guy with the absence of sex! This is the perfect way to make a man vulnerable to another woman's advances! You are not the only woman on this planet with a coochie (a slang term for the female sex organ). There is mega coochie walking in the street. There is plenty coochie at the office. Hell, everywhere you look there is coochie! So, what was the punishment again?

On one hand sex is a commodity. On the other, sex with a certain person is special. When you begin to punish a person with the absence of that experience, then you are belittling the act indirectly by saying it means more to him than it does to you. Conflicts and problems need to be dealt with head on, and not won at the expense of cutting off someone's supply of their favorite desert. People who win arguments that way will find that they either really didn't win after all or that their victimized person has found a NEW favorite desert, with someone who never puts a limit on their supply.

Ms. Jackson, ...if You're Nasty.
Question: Are you sexually adventurous and open to variety?

On one of the first radio shows I did entitled, "What Men Want", I interviewed women who specialized in sexual fantasy and in a day and time when some women are just trying to get a date, these women were booked every night. Many of their clients were already married. Why? We had a long discussion and I asked them this very question. And this is what they told me:

Bachelor Party Girl: I have several guys who come to me on a regular basis, so much so that they even bring me pictures of their wives and show me what they look like.

Anita: And what do they look like?

Bachelor Party Girl: Most of them are gorgeous! I look at these woman and think, "Why are you with me?" But I know the answer.

Anita: Well, what is the answer?

Bachelor Party Girl: I don't judge them. I provide sexual adventure and variety. It is what their wives won't do, that brings them to me.

And to that I say, "Ms. Jackson, if you're nasty!" Just as women like excitement, so do men. If you don't want to give him oral sex, maybe you should admit this, before you get married. If he is sexually adventurous before you get married, why would you think that he's not going to remain sexually adventurous after you get married. So, know what you're getting into.

Are you ready to compromise and change either your positions for having sex or the way in which you have sex? If you're married to a man who likes variety, do you really think that if you're not going to try, that he's just going to forget about it? If you married him and accepted to try to make the relationship work and grow, then that would include sex too. Right? Now, if you have tried something and didn't like it, or if you simply will not try something that he is insisting on, well maybe this is a marriage deal breaker (an item that would make closing the deal an impossibility). It is possible for people to change so much that they become different people, or more than you bargained for. We talked about how women can change, and men can do the same. When that happens, separation and divorce are always options. However, some men decide to stay with their wives (because it's cheaper to keep her) and just search for sexual gratification else where. If you're cool with the concept of a mistress for him, then more power to ya. But, don't be surprised if she starts to take on a more important role in his life.

It's Okay, If You Don't Inhale...

Question: When is it okay to have an extra affair or side fling? Is it okay, if it doesn't mean anything? Is it okay, if you didn't really enjoy it? Is it okay, if it was an accident and was unintentional? Or is it just plain okay...?

Gary was a red blooded man. He looked at women everyday. He loved looking at women. So, what's the big deal? What man can't appreciate a good-looking woman, right? He subscribed to Playboy, Penthouse and a few other magazine's that you probably have never heard of.

Gary fantasized about the women in his office and he rented those sexploitation movies all the time. He was into some different stuff that he said he had talked to his wife about, but that she wasn't interested in. So, he left her alone about it. My question is: "Is Gary cheating?" "He didn't have sex with any other women, but he fantasized, he thought about it a lot." So, is he cheating on his wife or is it only cheating when you actually go through the motions?"

I'm not going to give you the answer to that one; I want you to think about it.

However, some of the problems that married people have were there long before they get married; they just didn't surface, until now. This would include their reasons for getting married in the first place, and please don't say that they got married for "love"...you know how I feel about that word.

What Has He Done for You Lately!?
Question: The Mating Game takes the effort of two. Are you the only one trying?

The other day on an episode of MTV's LOVELINE a woman called in and said that she had done everything for her husband and she still could not get his attention or his interest. Regardless of what she did, he was more impressed with sports: basketball, hockey or football; he was a Sporty Scott (from the Chapter on Players). She never gained exclusive rights to his attention because as soon as one sport ended, another sport began. This is the kind of situation that can lead a woman to leave.

Just as a woman can leave the door open for another woman through the absence of sex (among other things), so can a man in leaving the door open for another man through the lack of spending his time, passion or attention with his woman. What did Ray Parker Jr. use to say back in the day, "A woman needs love, just like you do."

I think men need to be reminded on occasion that they've got a daytime job and a nighttime job, and if they can't handle the responsibilities of the position, women will be taking applications for a replacement. You've got to be careful though, because some men just look good on paper. However, in this woman's situation, despite all that she had done trying to get the mood started, her husband brought home a how-to-book on sex and told her that she needed to do what was in that book. The book was mentioned by name and I happened to be familiar with the content. However, listening to her, it appeared that she had tried many of the things that were noted in the book already, before the husband bought her the book! The problem here appeared to be that he was getting off scott-free from having to make any effort. He was putting the entire burden on her. All the effort was coming from her direction. So, what she needed to do was lay down the law and tell him the way life works. If it were me, I would have broken it down to him like this:

"It takes two, I can't put in enough effort for you and me both. You've gotten lazy and somehow come to the conclusion that it is solely my job to keep this relationship moving (sexually, intimately, communication-wise) and that is not only unfair, but I refuse to do it anymore. Secondly, if you can't at least put in an effort to do a better job at your nighttime job, I WILL be taking applications for your replacement. So, consider yourself on Notice, and this your official WARNING."

Closed Out

Question: Do you still have a life outside of your relationship?

One way that men control women is to keep them separate and apart from the rest of the world. Conversely, one way women allow men to control them is to permit themselves to be kept separate and apart from everybody. Can she go out to the movies? No, she has to cook his meals. Can she go out after that? No, she has to wash the dishes. Can she go shopping on the weekend? No, because she doesn't have any money. Can she get a job to make some spending money? No, she's got more than enough to do around the house and she's never done with that as it is. Can she get a job, if she can get all of her housework done? No, because no wife/girlfriend of mine is going to work.

Do you see how it works? She can never meet people; therefore, she can never find another man that can treat her better or offer her more (and believe me the options for better men are endless for this woman). Because most every man will be better than the one she has. She can't treat herself to a makeover or a new outfit; therefore, she will never attract another man when she has to leave the house to do the basic household necessities of the day. She can't ever go out; therefore, she can't make friends that would allow her to compare her life with the lives of others. Because, of course if she did, she would be unsatisfied with things the way they are and would attempt to either change them or leave. And of course, we can't have that. Because he likes things just the way they are.

If he controls her world, then he controls the way she thinks and he can control what is acceptable to her and what is permissible. This is the main reason I have a problem with older men getting into serious relationships with extremely younger women. Not because, I don't think they should date, but because the older man is working at an extreme advantage to the PYT (Pretty Young Thing).

He has been out and experienced life. She barley knows what affection is. She hasn't experienced a lot of relationships, so she has not set her standards yet in terms of what she will and will not accept in a man. These older men know that, and they therefore, know that these young women can be theirs for the picking by not offering much. That's how an 80-year old homeless man can get a 17-year old pretty, young girl, with the figure of Barbie.

She has had fewer experiences to compare her present experience to, and she is still in that state of mind believing that "love is all that matters". The problem with that statement is that she usually doesn't understand what "love" is, nor does she understand that it takes more than love to keep a relationship going strong. But how would she know this, this old warn out 80-year old man is the first serious relationship she's had, ever, and he knows it. And he knows that it is her lack of experiences that allowed him to get her in his life. However, no matter how much love she proclaims to have for him, it's an injustice to her.

Men that trap women in this method are no better than a school teacher that persuades an under aged boy to have sex (although there may not have been that much persuading needed). There's a reason why such things are illegal and there's a reason why it's considered "statutory rape" under the age of 18 years of age: lack of experience and limited ability to make a quality life changing decision (i.e.: pregnancy, marriage).

However, not every woman was trapped in this manner.

Understanding Nothing

You break-up. Things don't work out. Something must be wrong, right? Sometimes, we need desperately to believe that something is wrong with us. That's why our relationship didn't go well, we think. We tend to discard the possibility of "nothing" being wrong (with us).

I wasn't pretty enough! I wasn't nice enough! I wasn't attentive enough! These are thoughts that all come to mind when the blaring event of betrayal, lies and deceit come to a head. But sometimes, it's nothing that you could have done; nothing that you could have anticipated. Sometimes nothing could have changed this ending and what is wrong with you because it happened....nothing.

This entire premise of, "It's got to be something," comes from the belief that we have complete and total control over our lives. And while I believe that the general premise of the statement is true, the study of Logic teaches us that any statement including the term "never" is automatically false, because nothing is without exception. Therefore, any statement that you can make in your state of self-pity (if that is in fact where you are right now) is false as well. You know what I'm talking about. Things you say to yourself, conclusions you reach out of pain and hurt for your own sense of loss, like:

- I'll <u>never</u> find anyone like him.
- I'll <u>never</u> be happy again.
- I'll <u>never</u> get over this.
- Things will <u>never</u> get better.

From the simple fact that you included the word "never", automatically makes all of these statements false. There is always some possibility and always some probability that things will get better. Sometimes, things just happen. We control many elements, but we don't control everything. If we did, the end product would always be guaranteed, and it's not; that's why we refer to the whole thing as a game, because the stakes are uncertain. And if it's not the Mating Game you're playing, then it's the Game of Life. And although there is comfort in always knowing the end result, in either game, with the dismissal of pain would also go the dismissal of potential added joy. So, we continue to play both games, with the knowledge that we are playing the best way we know how and leave the rest to the way the chips may fall.

Welcome to the Players' Club

Why do women go after married or committed men? Because we are still playing someone else's game.

"Come on, baby. Don't be a Player Hater..."

Why do you think Ladies Night is free? Why do you think women wear tight fitting clothes that are not comfortable and show off every ass-et that God gave us? Why do you think women dance as though we are auditioning for a bed scene in a porn movie? Because women have been conditioned to believe through the course of conversation and through what they see, that this is what you have to do to get a good man (a man who will treat you right). We have been conditioned early on to play HIS version of the Mating Game, not our own.

Think back to high school. The boys wanted to have sex and the girls wanted to have dates. And if you had a boyfriend, well we all knew what you had to do to keep him. Remember the conversation that went on between most every couple?

"There are a lot of girls who would put out." he would say. "Do you want me to go to someone else?"

I ask you, have things changed much? No. Obviously, not. While the wording is different, the thought remains the same. Secondly, we are all led to believe that with age comes wisdom. But, that's not true. There are 18-year old mistresses and there are 55-year old mistresses. Obviously age didn't do anything for either of them. However, at least the 18-year old one has an excuse, for the moment. But in all honesty and out of respect for the youth of America, I have to admit that I have met several teenagers with more common sense about the Mating Game than some of the 40- and 50-year old women I have met. It's all the same game, whether you are a teenager or a 50-year-old woman. It's his game, if you allow it to be. And the object of the game is not to date, but to mate. Especially now.

Supply is Low!

"There aren't enough men, especially Black men!" one woman yelled out from the group. This is probably the biggest, most successful lie going yet. What? I know what you are thinking: "No, but it's true, Anita, the ratio of men to women in DC was 7 to 1 five years ago and now it's 12 to 1 and it's not just DC. The ratio of men to women is looking bad everywhere!"

Although statistics say that their are more women than men, visually I have not seen it. As a rule, I try not to put much faith, if any, in what statistics have to say. In fact, statistically all Black men above the age of 18 should be dead, but yet I "see" many Black men going to work everyday. However, I will admit that men, and African-American men in particular are getting too full of themselves. African-American men want me to believe that because of a statistical number, they can do anything and treat me any-which-way they so desire. Why? Because Black men are in HIGH demand.

It's SAD that African-American men want to use the fact that many African-American women would like to be with them, to our disadvantage, but as we learned earlier, nothing is absolute. So, to those FINE African-American men that are using and dropping those women like flies, I say: You aren't the only Black men in the world. Seventy percent of the WORLD is BLACK. And if that's not enough, the slave ship made MANY stops along the way before reaching America!

What does that mean to me? That means that there are Black Spanish men, Black Italian men, Black French men, Black Hispanic men, and we can't forget the Island Lovers (Caribbean men) and my personal favorite male, African Gold! The last African man I dated was well educated, spoke two languages, owned a 6 bedroom house, and had a job that sent him across the country weekly. Not only did he allow me to travel to visit him on the weekends, where ever he was, but he provided this also with the compliments of a limo. This man said that I was a Princess. Do you know why? Because he met my mother and he said that she was a

QUEEN. See, that's the kind of respect I'm talking ABOUT! A man that can appreciate and respect women as a whole is GOLDEN.

So, ladies, do not feel as though you have to stay or settle for African-American men that don't know how to act or someone who doesn't respect and appreciate what you have to offer, just because you're looking for a Black man. Because Black comes in many different flavors.

Would Somebody PLEASE Bring Me a Cocktail!

Kera was a friend from the old days. She had been very open about feeling that she was at a personal low. Things just go that way sometimes. So, we decided that she would come up for the weekend to relax and have fun. Well, the moment Kera walked through the door she said, "Would somebody PLEASE bring me a cocktail!

Relationships can be shitty! ...and life can pull some pretty hard blows. How many can you take at one time, and how do you deal with them? Sometimes people handle it by asking for a "bandage". A bandage is something you use to soothe an emotional wound. It's a temporary fix, a quick high. So, what do you use? We all use something. The problem begins, however, when we become dependent on those bandages and use them in excess. So, what's yours?

- **Alcohol**
- **Sex**
- **Drugs**
- **Money**
- **Work**
- **Food**
- **Exercise**

You're probably thinking, "Exercise? What's wrong with exercise?" Too much of anything is not good, even exercise. I'm sure you've heard of Anorexia (an eating disorder that causes individuals to stop eating and exercise excessively).

Bulimia uses food as a bandage along with exercise. The one exception of course being that you can eat all you want right before you make yourself vomit. Too much of anything is not a good thing.

It's not really the use of any of these items that makes them a bandage; it's the person's excessive use and dependence on the item to comfort them all the time that makes it into a bandage.

What do you think would happen if I took a crack head off the street and locked him in a house away from crack? Maybe, he would stop doing drugs. Maybe... This person would be more likely to find anything else in my house that would serve as a replacement bandage. Why? Because this is how they have been dealing with their problems. They have no intention of addressing them, so they look for a temporary bandage until they can rediscover their original bandage of choice. Because to come down off their high means that they have to deal with reality and pain, and that's the very reason that they are using the bandages in the first place.

An alcoholic who was trapped under house arrest has been known to start drinking rubbing alcohol. Why? A replacement bandage. Now, we can look at drug addicts and alcoholics and think that we are different, but when it comes to using bandages, how different are you?

- When you have a problem with work, is the first thing you do when you get home is have a drink? (You're using alcohol as your bandage.)

- When you have a rough argument with your husband do you run out only to end up in a bar and in another man's bed? (You're using sex as your bandage.)

- When you broke-up with your last boyfriend, did you grab a box of chocolates and a gallon of ice cream? (You're using food as your bandage.)

- Do you exercise excessively because you have a ferocious fear of getting older and becoming less desirable to your boyfriend? (You're using exercise as your bandage.)

Then you're using bandages too. The question is, "do you take the time to at some point stop delaying and address the real problem?" If not, maybe it's time you did. And the next time you feel compelled to use a bandage, ask yourself, "So, when am I going to deal with the real issue here?"

Now, you can use bandages to your advantage also. When you know that you will need a bandage to ease temporary relief, you can train yourself to pick ones that could help you over the long run. For instance: controlled exercise can be an excellent way to relieve stress. Painting or a hobby could be a great way to slowly work out an emotion. Talking to friends or family (about non-relationship related issues) can be a way to figure out a new plan of attack for a problem. So, you can actively attempt to use bandages to your benefit too.

Golden Guy

Just as we were talking about using bandages, guys have created there own special category of bandages to supplement a category of needs; I call them the "Golden Bandages".

Golden bandages are either sexual or relationship based in nature. They are used on an on-going basis to supplement a lack of sexual satisfaction or to meet a relationship-related need.

Previously in the book we discussed our Golden Girls as being need dependent and looking to supplement the important parts of who they are through men. Well, the Golden Guy is need dependent too, but instead of looking to his wife or girlfriend for his supplement, he goes to what I call the "Untouchables".

The untouchables are in a category by themselves. Placed on a pedestal, they are not truly considered to be real. The untouchables are untouchable because, in his mind he has built a fabricated fantasy or a history that makes the untouchables somewhat above imperfection. They are perfect.

The untouchables are difficult to compete with because, in some way, these women or people appear to be without fault. Their perfection is of course an illusion, but it is that illusion that fulfills the need and serves him in the manner needed.

Hotel Ho.

The Hotel Ho is the person on the street corner in your town who waits there every night for her regular guys to come buy (I did not misspell the word "buy"). They have sex in the car or go to a hotel; thus we have the name "Hotel Ho". Remember, an untouchable is someone who is an illusion, who is just what the person wants or needs them to be at that moment. What need is she explicitly satisfying? She provides and fulfills his secret sexual desires

His Boy!

The other man is his one serious guy friend that he is always hanging out with. His Boy is his confidant, his advisor, his sports companion and his comrade in playing the Mating Game. A man will talk to His Boy for the same reason a woman will tell her girlfriend her most personal secrets. There is a bond there that keeps these men attached and makes His Boy almost untouchable. The need that is directly being satisfied or provided is peer acceptance, staying a part of the single life, male emotional support, and friendship.

His Mother.

If we are going to talk about women who are outside of the reach of a wife, we have to include "his mother". No one can hold a candle to a man's mother. She clothed him, fed him and took care of him when he was sick. A mother is with a son for a lifetime, according to today's figures, a wife is with a man on average from 5 to 8 years (via marriage or the best of serious relationships). What need does she satisfy? She is security, emotional stability, longevity, continuous support, and affection.

Pin-up Babe.

This is the centerfold that men dream of dating. And I think it goes without saying that men use her as a frame of reference for the women they chose as well as to sexually satisfy themselves. We all know what they do with those pictures. These women provide eroticism and sexual gratification, and satisfy sexual curiosity.

Cyber Sex Slut.
This is a person acting under a hidden identity on the internet and satisfying sexual desires by way of computer sex. These women provide him with sexual fantasy without limits

Men who are seriously into their golden bandages are either using the bandages to fill in the missing elements in their relationships (through a variety sandwich) or is avoiding an important issue in his life that requires attention, such as:

- Having married a woman who doesn't like sex the way he does;

- Having become involved with a woman who doesn't provide enough emotional support;

- Having grown drastically apart in his existing marriage, but believes it's "cheaper to keep her"; or are

- Genuinely unhappy but stay together for the kids.

While the possibilities are endless, I'll let you fill in the other potential situations. However, I believe you get the picture.

Chapter 10

It's Not Over, 'Til It's Over...

■ ■ ■

I'm Going to Kill His ASS!

Whether it's a Jail Bait Mate replacing you or a Hotel Ho who has made the transition to real person, it's a painful thing to wake up one day and realize that you have slept years of your life away. Especially, if you wake up to discover that the man you had been dating or married to is not the man you knew.

It's as though he has been acting in a play for years and today was the day that you caught him for a brief moment, while he was out of character. You looked him in the face and realized that he was not the calm tempered, gentleperson you believed him to be. Instead, he was a vicious beast, laughing at your stupidity every step of the way and every moment of the day. So, now comes the anger, the hatred, and the feeling of loss. Questioning yourself with every shift of your thoughts:

- How could I have been so stupid?
- How could I have been so naive?
- How could it have taken me so long to realize all of this?
- Why didn't I question things more?
- Why did I believe everything he said, when he explained all of my concerns away?

So, now you feel used. Next comes the hate. The pain shortly follows, flowing down from every inch of your body. It consumes your every waking moment, your every free thought, day and night. It takes over your dreams at night and your spare moments when you drift during the day. Now, you're obsessed. You want REVENGE! But what kind of revenge does this world offer? Cheating is not a crime...not to the rest of the world, anyway.

So, you are left to wallow in your pain and hate, praying for retaliation, but there is none readily available for you to have. If you're married you think of getting the meanest attorney and demand more than half! You want everything! Take away his kids... If you were the girlfriend, you want his new relationship to end for him as painfully as yours did for you. You were the faithful one! You were the giving one! So who ended up hurt and left with NOTHING? You!

So, again your mind takes over and begins to plot devious methods of retaliation. But then you realize you are just living in a fantasy world. Because even though cheating is legal, murder is not. So, again you retreat within yourself with the pain, hurt and now the frustration of it all compounded by the absence of a way to vent it. This compounds the situation. ...while your mind constantly plots pain and misfortune for him to experience, with no legitimate way to feel redeemed. So, you grow madder and madder and angrier and angrier until it consumes your total being.

I Hate Him!

The only time anger can be dangerous, is when you allow it to fester inside of you destroying your confidence, among other things. Anger is really energy with no direction, and what a powerful form of energy! Imagine how many more stairs you can get in on the stair master machine when you think you can't climb another stair and then you immediately think of him and anger carries you up another four flights.

Can you imagine what you could accomplish, if you could direct that energy toward doing the things you want to do? Monster success! I am telling you, monster success!

So, back to our story. You are still pissed; so what do you do now? The answer is "forgive". Yep, that's right. I know exactly what you're thinking. "There is no way in Hell that I am ever going to forgive that miserable son of a ...b@#ch! I will hate and loath him for as long as I shall have breath in my body." ...right? You don't have to tell me, I remember. But before, you close the book, give me a minute to explain why you don't have a choice.

The Man Whom Hate Consumed.

A year ago, I was invited to sit in on a session during which men and women confronted people who had previously dumped them or done them wrong. While most of them had the usual "my boyfriend cheated on me" story, I met a man at a open talk and rap session in New York who had been angry for THREE years! I listened to him speak about what had happened. His girlfriend then came out and appeared to serve as his protector, because at that moment, he stopped talking and she became the voice that spoke on his behalf. While she was talking about his pain and his anger and the hurt that had been inside of him for the last three years, he sat there looking at the ground just completely tense from the pain, frustration, anger and the hate that he felt for this woman who had done him wrong three years ago.

The time finally came and wrongdoer came out; we will call her Jane. Jane was booed by everybody there, because of the graphic picture that her two predecessors had painted. When Jane sat down with the group, she didn't know why she had been brought there. When the two of them started attacking Jane about what she had done, she barely remembered the incident that happened three years ago. Still this man whom hate consumed, who had waited three years for this day, said nothing. His girlfriend confronted Jane and told her that she was an awful person for what she had done. His girlfriend went on to explain and complain about how Jane had ruined their lives for three years and how it still hadn't ended.

"He is permanently affected by all of this! I hope you're happy with yourself for what you've done to him!" his girlfriend concluded.

All the while, he sat bunched up in a ball, quiet, tense and in pain. After the session was over, I approached him. We spoke for a while about what he had experienced and then I asked him, "You say that you have been intensely angry with Jane for three years. Can you give me one example of anything good that has come out of your constant anger with Jane for this period?"

He looked at me funny for a moment and then I asked him again. "For three years without wavering, you have been consistently and bitterly angry with this woman, Jane. Obviously, it's doing something for you. Because, three years is a very long time to commit to one activity. So, I want to know one good thing that has come out of your anger with Jane?"

He thought about it for a second and then a bit longer and still a bit longer and then he said, "Well, nothing, of course, it's been a very painful experience for me?"

"Obviously. However, has it also been a painful experience of three years for Jane?" He didn't respond. I think it was the first time that he had thought about it.

I then asked him who was causing him to remain angry for such a long period of time?" He looked at me funny again. And then he finally said, "I don't understand all of these questions."

Then I told him. He had been wronged by this woman. He was so hurt by the situation that he decided: "I will never forgive her." Now, three years had passed and for three years he had been so angry about it, that it had directly affected his life negatively in every aspect including his personal relationship with his girlfriend. However, it was not until that very day that his anger even once touched Jane.

So, why was I asking him all of these questions? Because, I wanted him to see that his anger of three years continued to live because of his inability to forgive. And while his desire to never forgive this woman, Jane, was an attempt on his part to hurt her forever, the only person that he had been hurting on a daily basis had been himself.

It was not until that day that Jane even realized the impact that a moment three years ago had even made on his life. But by that same token, do you think Jane is going to go home and not be able to sleep at night because of the forgiveness that this man was unwilling to give her? Absolutely, not. This man had admitted to me that sometimes he'd been so angry that he couldn't sleep, he couldn't work, and he wouldn't go on outings with his girlfriend. Why? Because he was too busy sitting in a chair being intensely, obsessively ANGRY with Jane, who was 2,000 miles away in another state, and completely unaware of his anger.

You forgive not because the person who did you wrong is a good person. And, it's definitely not because the person who did you in was right. It's because forgiveness is actually a very selfish thing. You don't necessarily forgive to free someone else from the guilt, hurt and pain, and you definitely don't forgive to allow someone back into your life to hurt you in the exact same manner again. You forgive to free *yourself* from the guilt of not being perfect, of not having protected yourself and of not having known.

When to Say, "When!"

This question is asked everyday. Somewhere today there is at least one woman sitting in front of a mirror looking at her own reflection, thinking, "Is this the day that I call this relationship quits?'

What a difficult question to answer. When do you know it is time to quit?

- When you feel you have put in an honest effort.
- When you feel he no longer cares (you can't make somebody else care or try to make it work).
- When you feel that the relationship is taking away from you, not giving and there is no reasonable answer in sight of correcting the problem.
- When you feel the relationship is not moving forward and it's now moving backwards, taking you along with it.
- When you've talked to him and your goals are so different that in order for you both to accomplish them, you would both have to be on separate paths.
- When you are happiest when you're away from him.

- When the absence of his presence breathes a sigh of relief into you that can only be equated to a release of pressure and the absence of pain.

It may sound obvious, but it's not. In order to really ask yourself these questions, detach yourself from the problem. Pretend that you are somebody else and ask yourself, "What would I tell a friend to do?" And that's the answer you should give to yourself.

When is it Time to Make a Change?

Tina had been abused by Ike for years. So, what made her fight back one day? Don King had heard about boxing many times before, yet why was the one moment when he heard a fight on the radio while moping in jail, so different from all the other boxing fights he had listened to? No one has an answer that is absolute for everybody, but for some reason, you can listen to the same lecture over and over and there is just one day when it all clicks for you. Despite the dozens of times you tried to understand, this time is different for some reason, and this time you decide to make that change.

Anthony Robbins, calls it reaching your "pain threshold". As he explains it, up until that point you are in the middle. Things are not that great. You're not really happy, but you're not really unhappy either. You're in a sort of emotional limbo that's not really one or the other; so it's acceptable. Things, for you, still haven't gotten to the point were the pain just becomes so unbearable that change becomes mandatory.

Tina had become comfortable with the daily pain and emotional abuse of Ike, but what caused her to fight back on that day, at that moment? In later years, Tina explained that at that time in her life, her children had left and were no longer in the picture. The fear of her children growing up without a home because of her actions was now no longer a potential consequence of leaving. In general, the pain of leaving became less than the pain of staying. But change does not always have to be prompted by circumstance.

People have the ability to change at any moment and be the person they want to be. It is not a miraculous thing that occurs overtime. If you really wanted to, you could make all the changes that you have ever wanted to right this very moment. You could sit down and make plans to be the person you have always wanted to be. If you took a moment right now to write down what you wanted in life, and where you would like to be, then stop and think: how to get there? With just one small step every day toward your goal, just think of where you could be one year from now, two years from now, five years from now! The possibilities become endless.

Consistently making the required effort daily, you will see change and progress in the direction that you have chosen to go. Make it a rule that everyday you must do at least one thing, complete one real activity that moves you forward. If you did just one thing a day, one year would equal 365 changes. What a difference a day makes.

Value Your Emotional Anchors.
Emotional Anchors are the weights that keep us true to who we are. When the tides of turmoil hit (relationship or otherwise), it's the emotional anchors that keep us roughly in place. These anchors are based on four type of relationships

- Family
- Peer Relationships
- Individual
- Nurturing Relationships

Family is the first type of relationship we experience. From developing strong relationships with parents, siblings, cousins, aunts and uncles, we develop anchors that include a sense of security and stability through unconditional love. Also, we learn by the example of our family what a really committed relationship, like marriage, should be. However, if we don't acquire the anchors family relationships are intended to bring to our lives, then we tend to be swept away with the tides of turmoil. We permit others to change our life, because we fear the lack of stability or security. If we have learned anything from a negative family relationship it is that the "fear of a lack of security" can place us in a series of bad relationships in our adult life.

From peer relationships, we experience our first encounters with person to person interaction, one on one. Our first such experience is having a best friend. These relationships offer us a sense of feeling accepted. Hence, through the standards of others, we acquire beliefs similar to, "I must be okay, because people like me." We experience the desire to be "liked" because that would mean that we not only meet everyone's perception of normal, but we exceed it. We establish an understanding of what conditional acceptance means: to be liked based on a set of predetermined norms. From these experiences, we develop anchors that make us feel accepted based on society's expectations. People who haven't acquired these anchors will find themselves changing to fit into someone else's definition of what is acceptable or exceptional in a person, like beauty is for a Beautiful Betty. These conditional factors are the very reason that a Chameleon Camele is always changing. She's changing to fit what's acceptable.

Individual is the term used to describe the relationship we have with ourselves. This is when we attempt to better understand and help ourselves in reaching our own personal goals. Many women who avoid spending time with themselves are generally the ones who end up later running away from a marriage and three kids to FIND themselves.

Most people underestimate the value of spending time developing a relationship with themselves. Women who under-value the worth of appreciating their own time, their own brilliance, their own contributions, have ended up unhappy because they expected their husband or boyfriend to constantly reinforce her sense of individual value, which is not fair to him. Nor is it a realistic substitute for your own admiration of yourself and your own acknowledgement of your true value.

A nurturing relationship is what a father/mother experiences with a child. It is the reaffirmation that our experiences can help others. From this, indirectly comes a stronger valuing of self along with the belief that individual life has impact.

Take an Emotional Vitamin Everyday.
Just as it's important to take vitamins daily to strengthen the body, it's also important to take vitamins daily to strengthen your emotional well being. Emotional vitamins are what we need to help build up our emotional immune support system. It's what's needed to fight off negative words or actions and are used to control life crisis when it occurs. Just as a regular vitamin when taken in advance, emotional vitamins serve to prevent future illnesses or setbacks and if taken in the wake of a crisis, they tend to help improve your emotional recovery.

An emotional vitamin is something that enriches your mind and thereby affects your emotional disposition. It's merely the act of taking something in that's positive to your mental state, like reading a section in a book or reading a verse in the Bible or the words of Allah. It's taking a moment to be with yourself and just ponder on thoughts and positive ideas or a moment of silence for meditation and reflection. It could be a fun moment playing with your children or quiet moment with your boyfriend or husband. It really doesn't matter what it is, just as long as it impacts your mental state positively.

I'm sure that you've experienced days when you felt down and didn't know why. It was not a physical illness, it was just a general overall feeling of depression, discontent or unhappiness. It's what happens when you neglect to take your emotional vitamins.

Whose Opinion Matters?

When you're in the middle of crisis, people can use some hard words to eat away at every bit of confidence you've harnessed. Although the bad stuff isn't true and people are just using words to tear you down, it seems to always be easier to believe the bad stuff. A person can tell you, "You're worthless, stupid and ugly," do you believe them? Whose opinion has more value? His or yours?

I went church hopping (visiting a variety of churches) last October, and fell upon a sermon given by a very well known pastor. He was so well known, that his sermons were generally televised every Sunday. And although I am slightly ashamed to admit it, sometimes my mind drifts when listening to sermons. It usually happens when I feel that what the pastor is talking about doesn't apply to me, or if I get preoccupied with a concern or a thought. This time, I was drifting because I was thinking about a long list of things I needed to do once I got home.

They say that the mind is always listening, it merely selects those things that it believes you will be interested in and ignores the rest; the term for this is selective perception. It must be true, because I was deep into thought about a list of to do's when I was immediately pulled out of this state by one sentence given by the pastor. He said, "Your body parts determine whether you are a man or a woman, but you can't be both."

I snapped to attention and immediately thought, "Has he met Ru Paul?" This man then went on to say that, "If God creates all things, as he does, and he created these people [anyone other than a heterosexual person], then God must be a fool."

I couldn't believe he had just said that, but it was obvious that this pastor, this man that had studied the bible for longer than I had been alive, believed what he was saying was true.

Dr. Spock, several years ago, was known as the Baby Doctor. He was the epitome of knowledge concerning children. People all across the country were raising their children based on Dr. Spock's advice. Then years later people discovered that Dr.

Spock didn't have all the answers, but he believed he did.

Several years ago when my brother was little, he had a medical problem. My mother took him to a doctor and the doctor told her that if my brother didn't have an operation immediately, he may never have a normal life. My mother refused and in a short time the problem corrected itself and he has never had a problem since. The doctor didn't have all the answers, but he believed he did.

Dick Gregory, a well known entertainer, nutritionist and author, has openly admitted many times that he use to be an avid drinker, among other things. One day he decided to stop drinking alcohol, started drinking water every day and began fasting once a week. Dick Gregory told people that his doctor was completely against it at the time. Thirty years later, someone approached Dick Gregory and asked him, "How does your doctor now feel about your fasting every week for 30 years?" Mr. Gregory replied, "I don't know; he's been dead for 28 years." Dick Gregory's doctor didn't have all the answers, but I'm sure he thought he did.

I tell you this to show you a few things. No one has all of the answers. A doctor can claim to know more than the average person, but he/she does not know it all. People have experiences and it is up to the person to extract meaning and learning from those experiences. Doctors and experts alike claim to know more because they have accelerated their exposure to a variety of experiences through studying the work of others. We participate in a similar activity when we talk to friends, family parents and read books to expand our own base of knowledge, again through the experiences of others, but we still don't know it all. And it is through these experiences that we establish our understanding and the concepts that form our belief system.

Questions are answered based on what we believe and it is what we believe that dictates our decisions and that indirectly affects the type of life we will have: the type of relationships we will have. Others can give you opinions and thoughts to help broaden your views, to expand your knowledge and learning, but only you can make the decisions that will impact your life. So, let's talk about perception.

Come Over To My Side.
Last summer, I was driving my car, when I decided I really needed to check the oil. When I got out of the car and tried to open the car's hood on the passenger's side, the hood would not budge. I couldn't believe it. I tried for at least 5 minutes and the hood wouldn't move. Because I couldn't check the oil, I was afraid to drive the car (I was afraid of damaging the car). So, out of a lack of options, I made plans to have it towed into a shop. However, a few days before that happened, my brother happened to come into town. He asked if he could help me with anything and I jokingly said, "Yes, you could help me get the hood of my car up."

Going out to the car, I released the hood. I stood on the passenger's side (the same place I stood before) and he stood on the driver's side. I started by showing him the problem, I pulled and nothing happened.

"You see" I said as I pulled harder on my side, "the hood will not budge." And with that, and no effort what so ever, he lifted the hood up...from the driver's side. I stood in amazement. There was no problem with the hood. Out of disbelief, I walked over to the driver's side by him closed the hood and then attempted to open it again. It opened! It opened easily. It was as though the entire problem was only in my head. And that's why this section is called, "Come Over to My Side".

If you think of a relationship or a problem as a 3-dimensional image, to truly understand what you are looking at, you would need to walk around it to see it from a few different angles. A relationship is no different. If you never change your position and hold fast to an unwavering stance, how could you ever expect to see anything differently. That's why I say, "come over to my side": move from the same spot you have occupied and look at your situation from a few different angles.

Think about it. Imagine if you were standing in the dark what a statue would look like. Viewing it from the same position day after day is the same thing as having one perception about your relationship. When friends, family or you, for that matter, bring new elements into the picture which might make you have to question your perception; you resist and decline to budge from your one view. What is happening here? It means that you are seeing and hearing only what you want to; you are being selective in your perception. You are selecting what you will and will not include within your perception. Why? Because, you like the view you've got just fine. To change your current position would be to challenge your existing perception and that might cause uncertainty, pain or discontent.

If you look at this symbolic example for it's representation: the light represents new information to help you see the item clearer. If the object is as it appears, then the light will not change how the object looks. However, if you have been deceived, due to the darkness (also referred to in this scenario as a lack of information that you would not acknowledge) then the statue (your relationship) will look differently from viewing it in the light and from a different position.

Challenge yourself with information and operate from a position of strength.

Ultimatum vs. Broken Promise.
There are many Dominant Donnas who say, "See what I did! I told him, 'Get it together, or I'm leaving this crap!" Time then passes, he doesn't get it together and she doesn't follow through with her ultimatum. Now, he knows he can do this all the time and nothing will happen. His cheating becomes

a joke. There is no consequence for his or her lack of commitment. And so, he cheats again and again. Why not? There is no consequence for his actions. An ultimatum without follow through on the consequence is nothing more than a broken promise.

Repetition Can Be Dangerous.
It is important to know that the same things that can build you up and give you power can also tear you apart and destroy you.

Do you remember when you were little. Did your mother or father call you a smart little child or a dumb ass bastard? It's a very valid question. Why? Well, whichever you were called, do you remember being called it a lot? If you did, did you then begin to believe that you were what your mother or father said you were? Yes, you did. Why? Because just as repetition can build you up, it can tear you down. It's a self-fulfilling prophecy. It doesn't have to be true, but with repetition, you believe it into reality.

Second question, do you really think the function of your brain has changed so dramatically since then that a similar pattern wouldn't have the same affect on you? No, it hasn't.

Repetition is a powerful tool. It's part of the sword of communication which cuts both ways. So, how do you undo the voodoo? The same way you did it. If you think of it slightly from a mechanical point of view, for every one time that you heard or were told something negative you need to counter it with the opposite statement. And you have to continue this process until you have an equal number of counter statements on the other side of the scale to equal the same number of negative comments made.

Then you need to go one more on the positive side to make the scales tip in the direction of the positive perception, and that is when the mental perception will change, when the positive comments outweigh the negative ones in number and in intensity. It may sound really complicated and lengthy, but Hell, you all ready went through the process one time to mess up your life. The least you can do for yourself, is go through the process a second time to correct it. It's not as though you really have anything else more important to do. If you work from the perspective that you only have one life to live, what are you thinking, you are too busy to do this for yourself in this life. So, you will just not do the negative stuff in the second one? The process is really not as bad as it sounds, and I guarantee that if you sincerely make an effort, you will see some wonderful changes.

Plant some positive seeds in your mind. You've given the weeds the run of your brain for a while. So, pull the weeds and give the good plants at least equal time. They deserve a chance to grow too.

Not Everyone Was Meant to be Married

This may not be a popular thought. However, there is a hidden strength in allowing yourself to just be who you are. There is a power in recognizing and accepting that each day offers it's own set of challenges and excitement.

I met a 32-year old woman once at a friend's party who was so intent on getting married that she had a plan of action. You may think, "oh that sounds like a reasonable idea," but the idea had gotten so out of control, it was in the scary mode. I met her through a social event, she seemed nice enough. So, we started talking on the phone about things in general. It seemed to be a mutually beneficial relationship because, she was keeping me up with the social events in town and I was giving her an ear to talk to. Well, don't ask me where things started to take a turn. I suppose there never is one situation or conversation that can be summed up to the actual turning point to prompt the scene of the crime, but after telling me that she had her heart set on getting married she turned into something slightly short of Glenn Close from *Fatal Attraction*!

She said she had goals and one of them was to be married by age 28. She had attended every major social function searching for an eligible African-American man in Chicago and she was running out of time.

"I am suppose to be married by 28, Anita. That means I need to be engaged by 27 and I am 26 NOW, without any prospects."

I tell you it was not for a lack of trying. This girl had been everywhere, met everyone, dated any potential one, but still not met "The One". The calls initially started coming every week. After a while, they began to intensify and she was calling me every other day. I moved to a different state, far, far away and still, the calls kept coming! I know what you're thinking and shame on you; I didn't move because of HER. I didn't need to, I was a woman. I didn't have anything to fear from her. It was MEN who were in trouble! And this was getting scary, not because she was calling, but because the conversations during the calls were becoming more and more intensified.

"I don't know what I'm doing wrong! I went out with this fine guy. He said he was interested, but when I tried to call him, I found that he was not taking my calls! He's too busy for me. He has got other things to do! Yep, right... I don't know what the HELL he thinks I am? But, I'll be damned if he does this to ME!!" she yelled over the phone in a voice of disgust, betrayal and panic. Then she converted back to her initial state and continued, "You know I have a goal of being married in two years, Anita. I read a book and it said that you have to plan for what you want and make what you want in your life happen! And that is exactly what I am trying to do, Anita. I have a goal of being married, so I intend to be married. I am doing everything.

Everything! And still it doesn't seem to be working. I don't understand it. I should be well on my way to being married, but instead I feel as though I am still on square ONE!!" She was starting to lose it again.

I tell you about her story only because, I wanted to show you how much pressure it can be to try to MAKE things happen. Not everything is meant to be. Maybe you'll get married, maybe you'll just have great sex with several lifetime lovers. Maybe you'll get married at 28, maybe you'll get married at 40. You can try to make things happen, but there are no guarantees that it is going to happen in your time frame and in your perceived manner. And that is exactly what she wanted. She had a plan of action, an objective and it was suppose to come to a resolution by the time she turned 29.

Talk about pressure. She was stressing herself out so much, that she couldn't even think straight. If she had met some special guy, I guarantee you that she scared him off by being so demanding. "This must happen now! And this must happen later!" she would say. That was her way of thinking, and unfortunately, you can try and of course your chances can improve with effort; however, there is a breaking point at which more effort is just self-defeating and girlfriend was well past that point.

Her attitude was wrong. Undoing years worth of frustration was not something that could be achieved in a few minutes. But, she needed to slow down. Girlfriend was so focused on winning the race, that she had forgotten to enjoy the ride.

Why are we in such a hurry to get THERE? Where's there? You know. THERE? Marriage, as though marriage is some fairy tale land where when you walk through the door someone yells, "...and they lived happily ever after." I know about as many UNHAPPILY married women as I know HAPPY single ones.

Ladies, you need to adapt an "I'm happy with what I've got and if I get more, I'll be happy too" attitude! Don't expect happiness to come in the form of the same recipe for everybody. Happiness for you may not include marriage. It might include a house on the beach in Miami with a live-in lover that's half your age, when your 50. Happiness for you could be 2 failed marriages, but 3 wonderful kids and 5 beautiful grandchildren.

If your rushing to get happiness in the same form as everyone else because you believe that it only comes in one form, then maybe you will not be available when your real happiness comes along. Your happiness might be a new love interest every year, while you travel the world and live in France. Happiness does not come in a ready to make package. It is a different recipe, with a list of different ingredients made especially for different people. So, stop forcing yourself to fit into a mold that was not necessarily made for you. Concentrate on being happy and the rest will fall into place.

The Breakup Rules

1. When it's over, let it be over.
Now this doesn't mean that it couldn't be back on later, but at this moment, it's over. So, don't cling and don't hang-on.

2. Look Good.
There is nothing more irritating for the Ex than to see you looking good and feeling good. It belittles their impact on your life and also makes them question letting you go.

3. Leave when you're ready.
Although there are a million people I would like to see get out of their current scenarios, if you leave because everyone says you should leave, then you will either be right back shortly or find someone else to provide the same set of circumstances. So, in order to avoid this, as painful as it is, we need to leave when we are ready.

4. Work on one thing.
It's not that you need to strive to be perfect. However, we put more effort into improving our professional status than we do on improving our personal mental/physical status.

After the breakup, find one thing about yourself that you could feel good about improving and work on it. This takes your focus off the breakup and gives your mind something to think about. It also makes you stronger for the next go round in the Mating Game.

5. Jump back into the Game!
When you fall off the horse, it is mandatory to get back on. The same is true here. One bad go round in the game doesn't mean that it will always be that way.

6. Change Your Game Plan.
The problem with playing the Mating Game is that few decide to challenge the game. We look at it and decide we either need to jump in the game or evoke some serious massive change. All the while, most of us end up losing because we are not playing for the things we want or because we are playing the game by someone else's rules. When we do it this way, typically we end up hurt only to hear someone say, "Hey, don't be a player hater!"

Perfecting Your Game Plan

Within the real life examples stated in this book, there have been several common problems. The main one being that people didn't create their own set of rules to let others play by and or when their playing of the Mating Game resulted in a negative outcome, they didn't make changes to the way they decided to play the game the next time.

One woman who provided her experiences, after several heart-wrenching stories of her failed outcomes, showed me letters that she had written to herself back in college addressing what she was doing wrong in her relationships with men. The unbelievable truth is that what she had written to herself as a wake up call five years prior could not have been more true in the present. Despite what she had written, she had not changed her game plan one inch. It was as if she had written the letters only yesterday.

So, constantly challenge the way you're playing the Mating Game, in the beginning, during the game and especially after the breakup. If you challenge your game plan, and make adjustments and changes along the way and after each play, you eventually will come up with a plan that works for you… in the Mating Game.

Peace!…I'm out of here!